This Book Belongs To

Copyright ©
JACHICO PRESS
All Rights Reserved 2022

Coloring Test Page

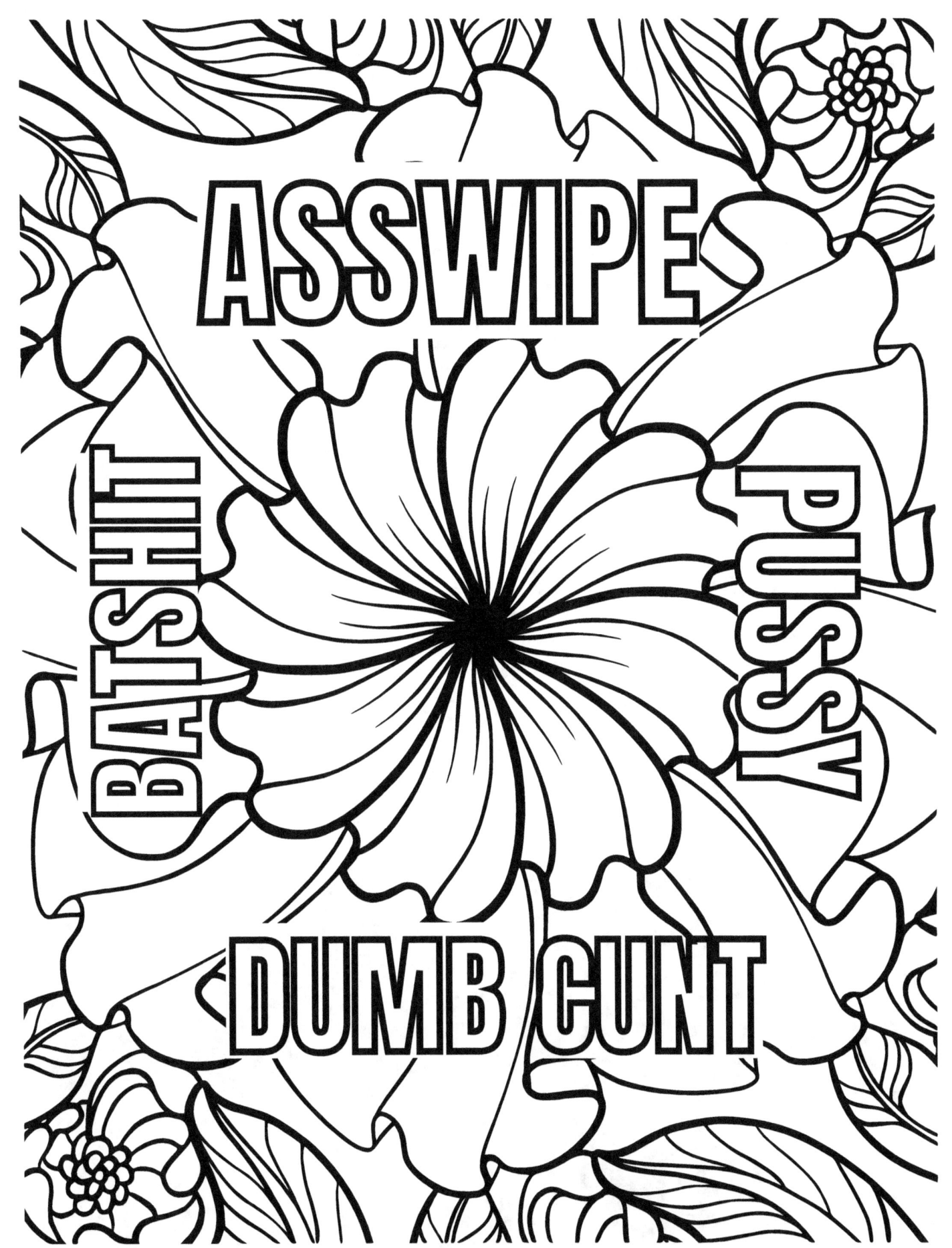

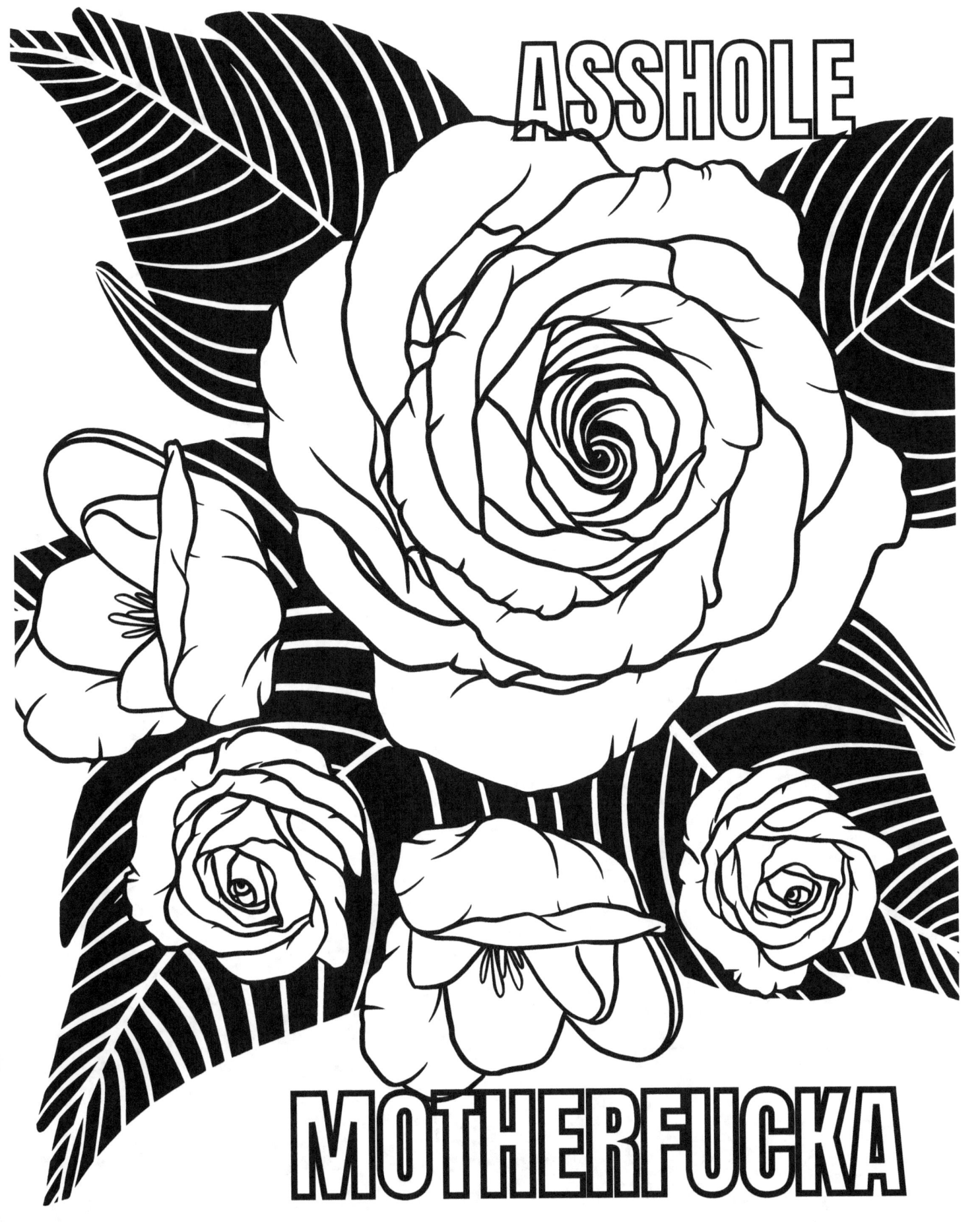

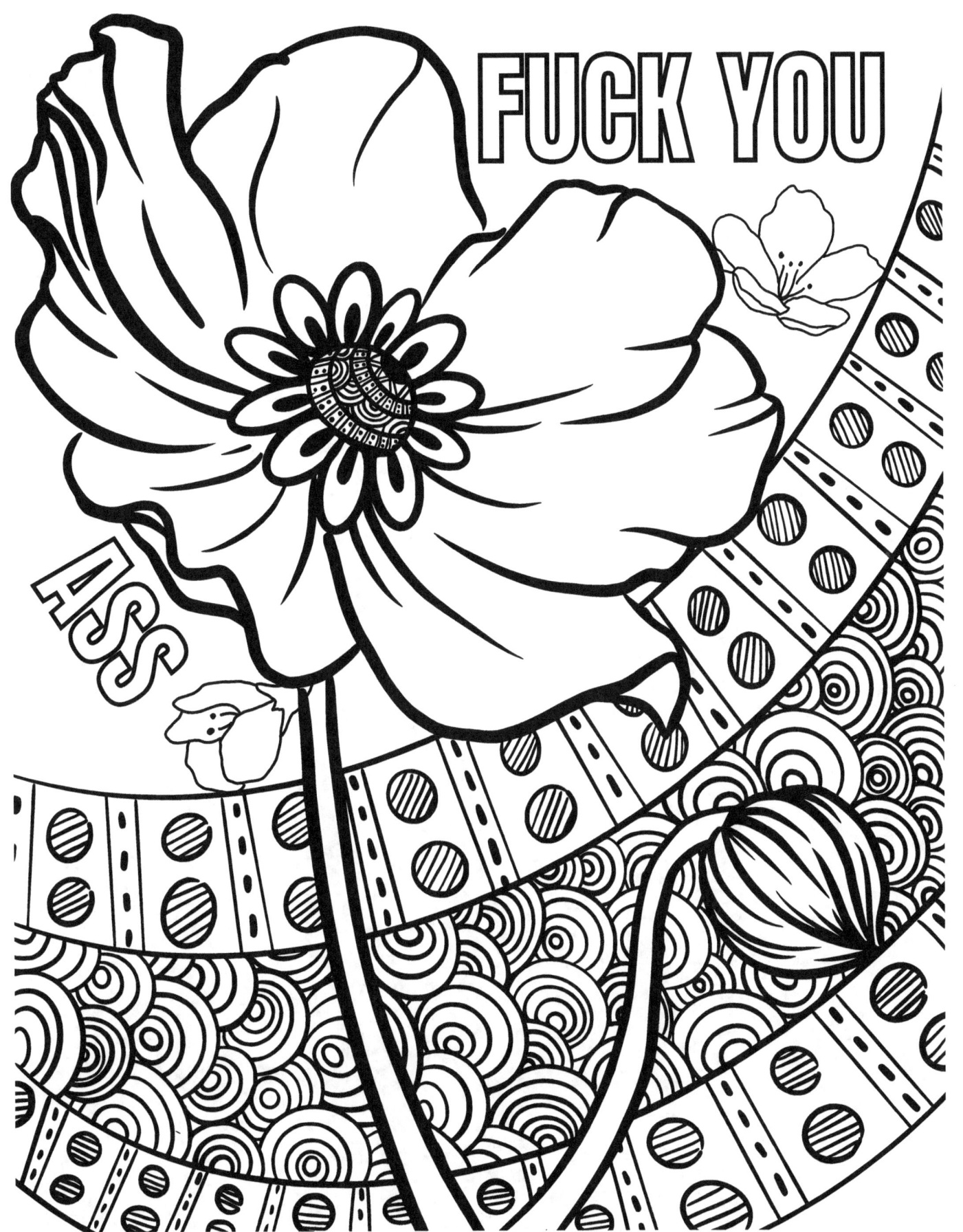

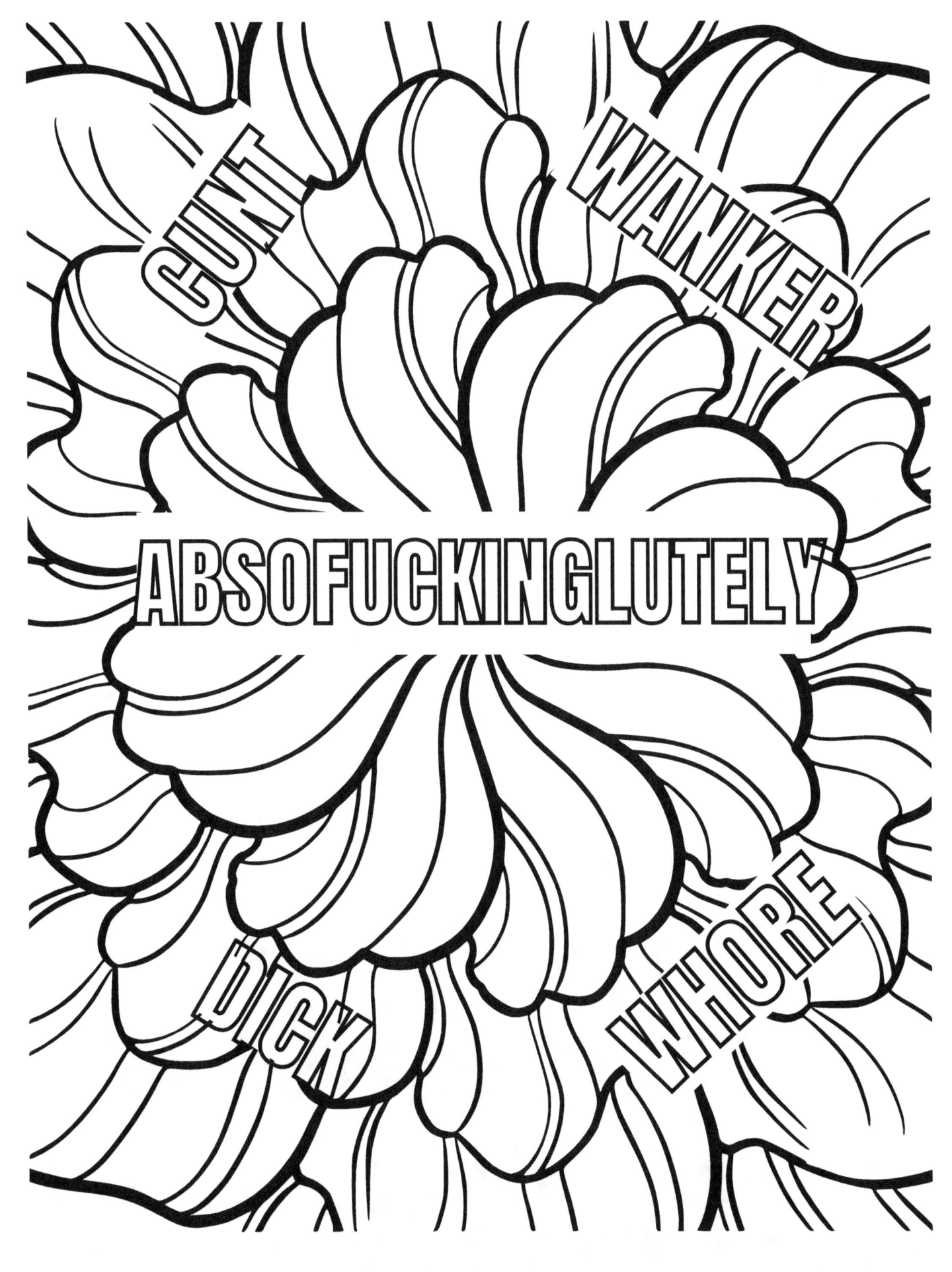

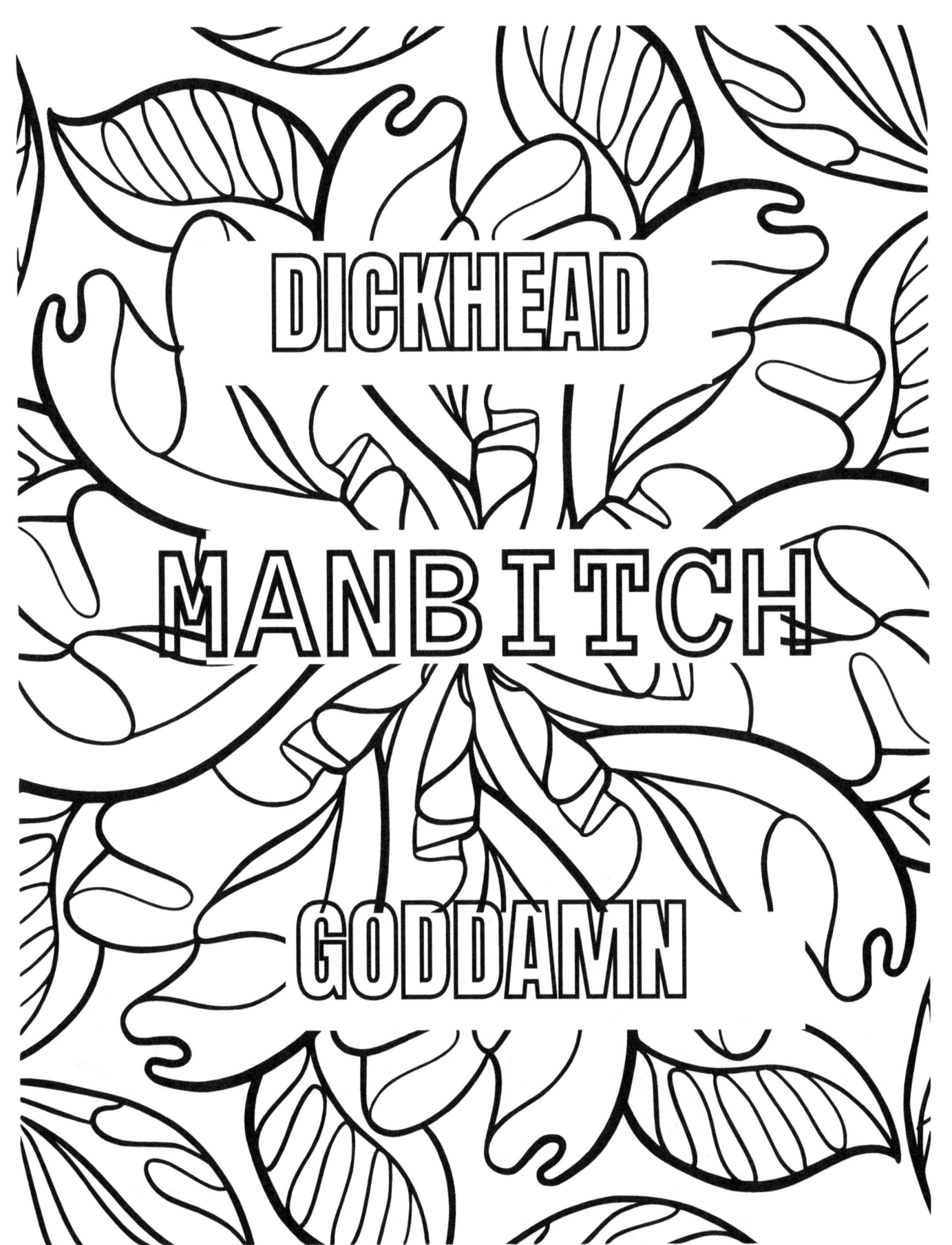

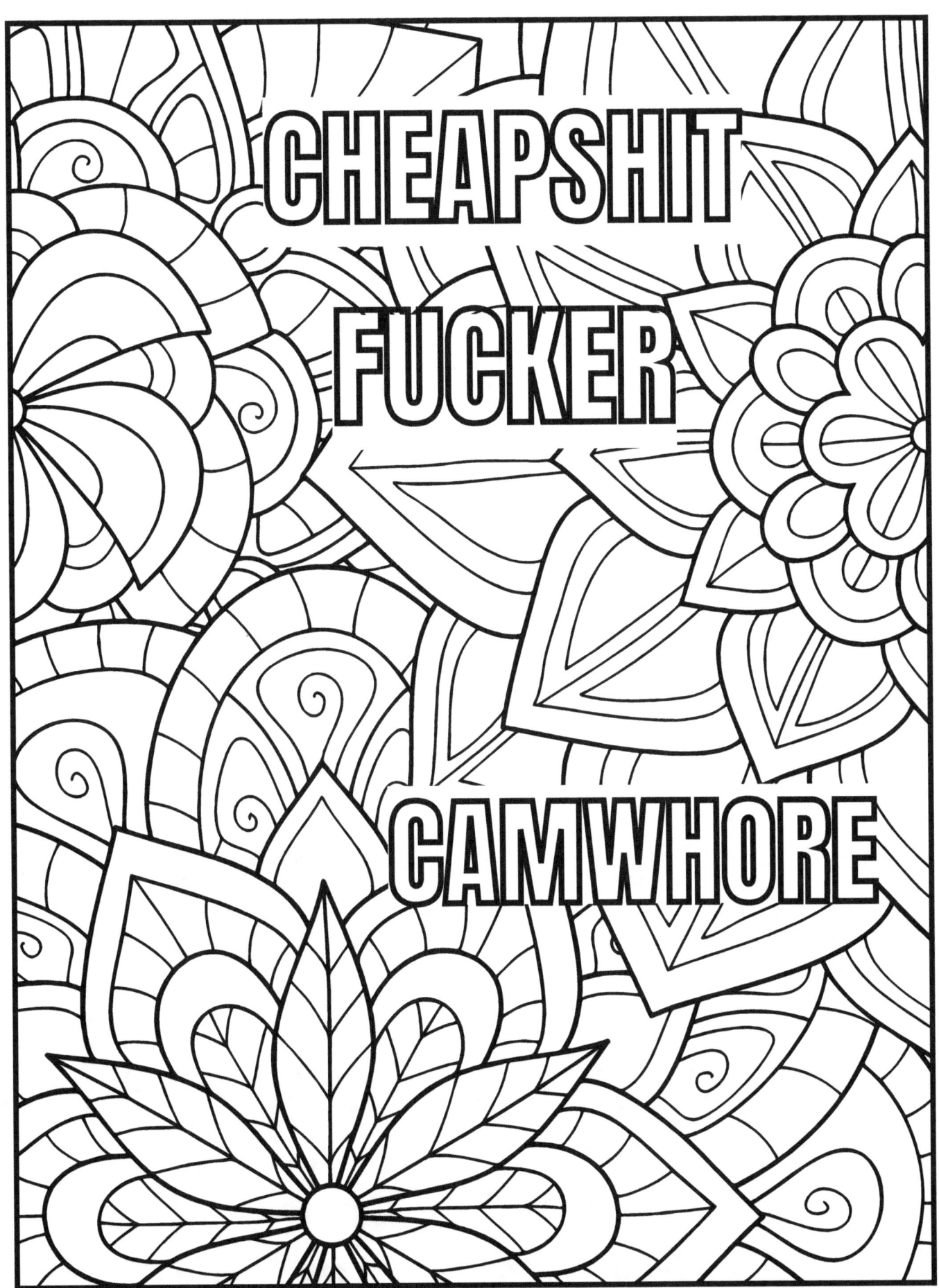

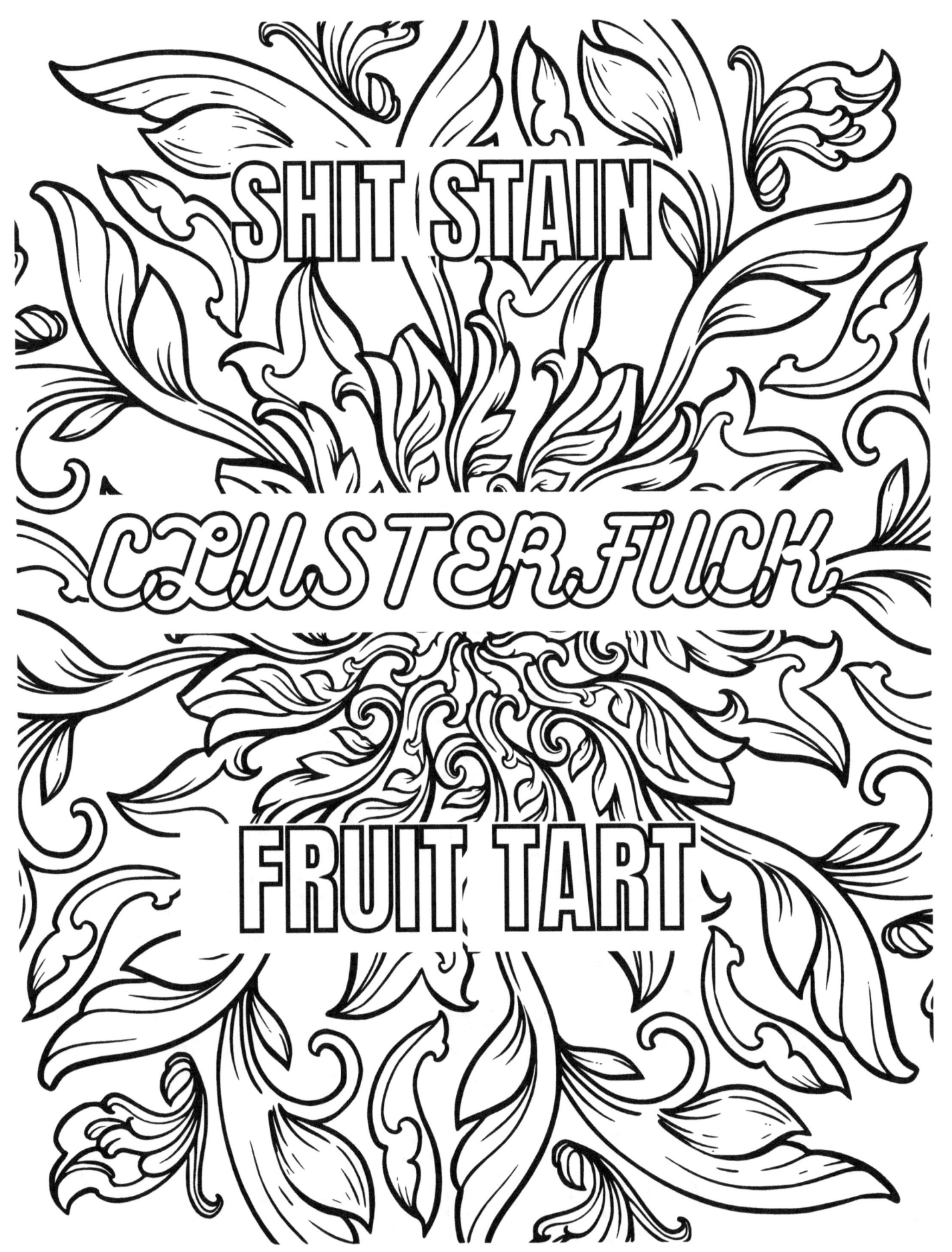

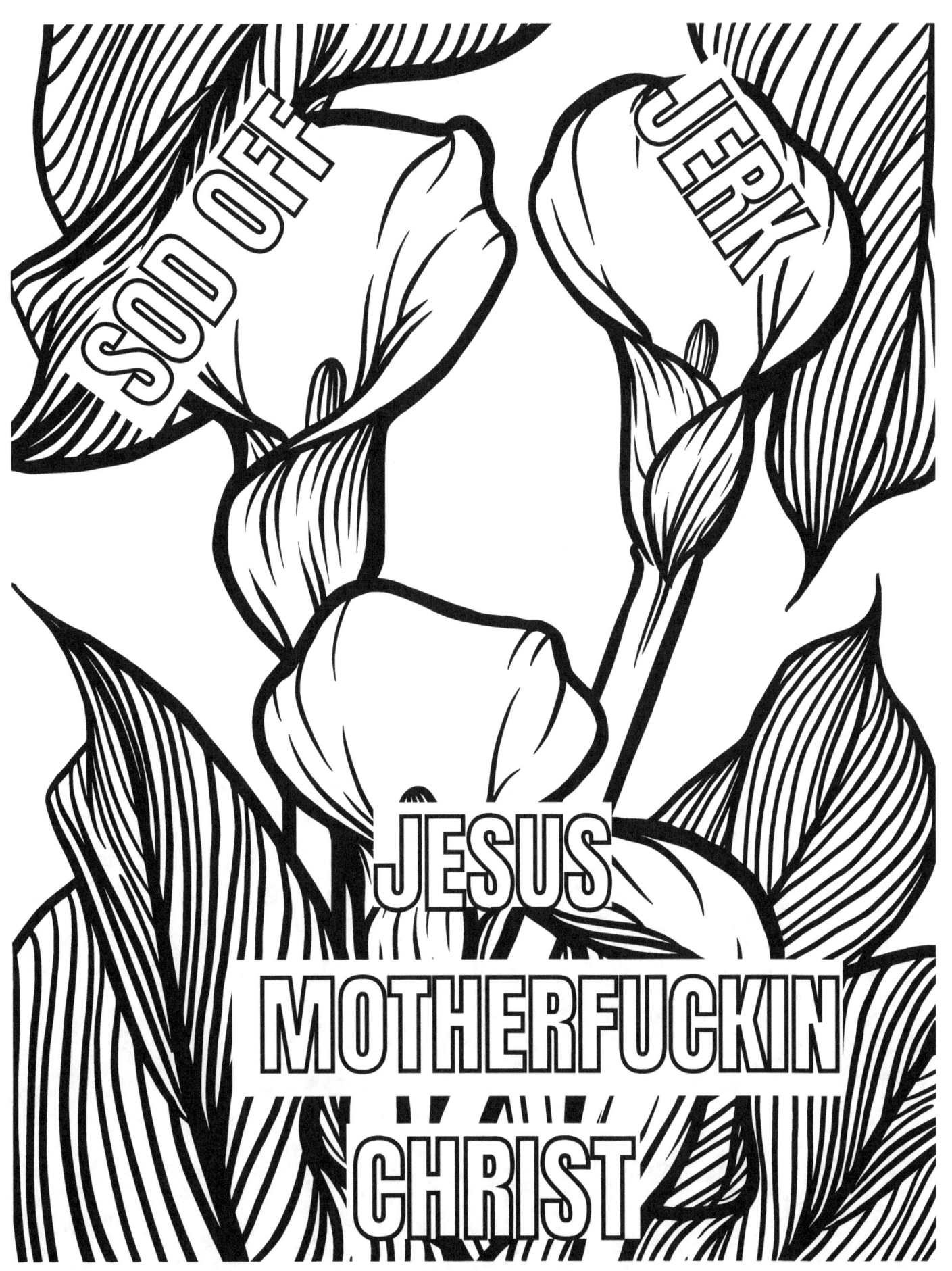

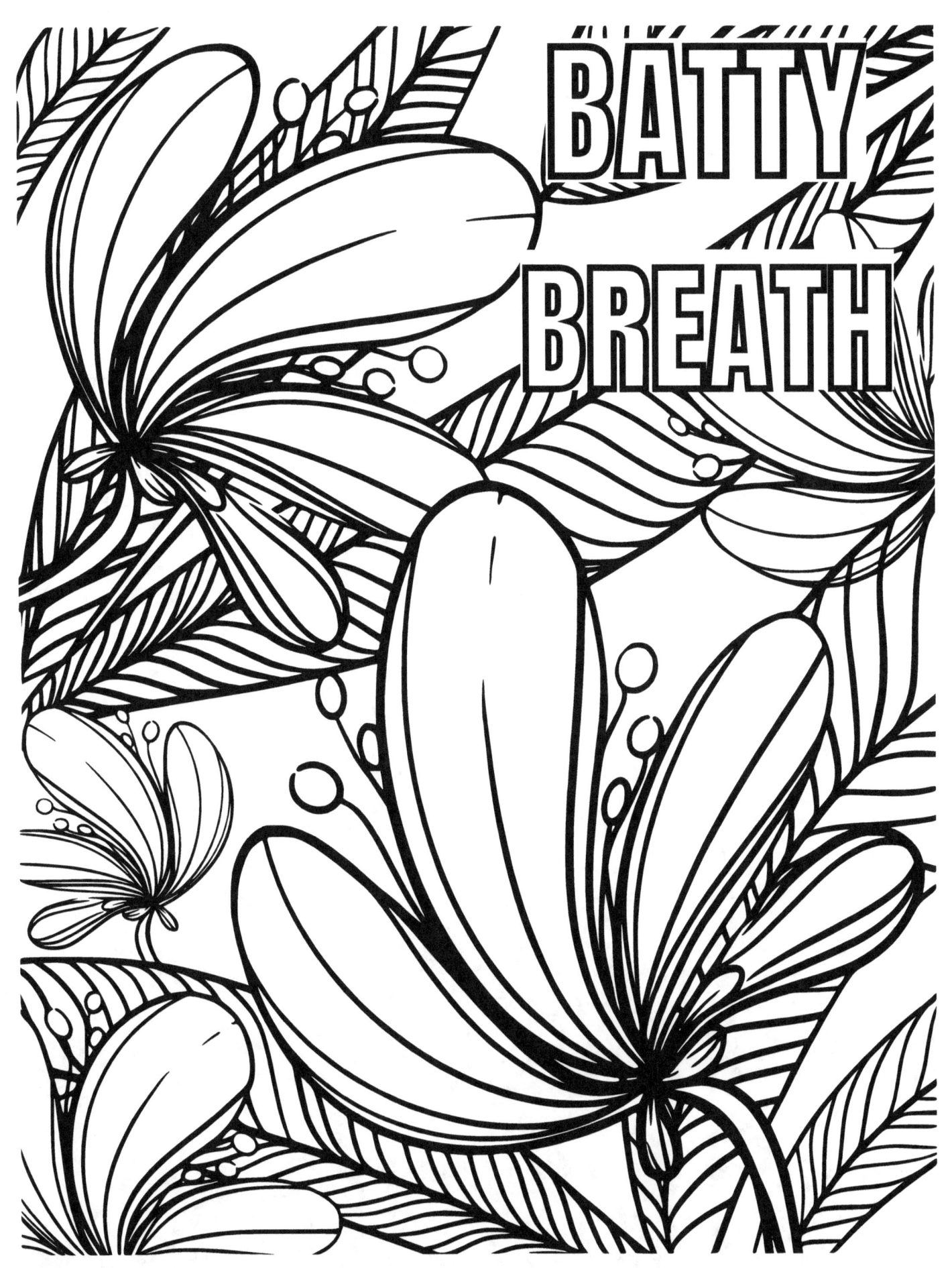

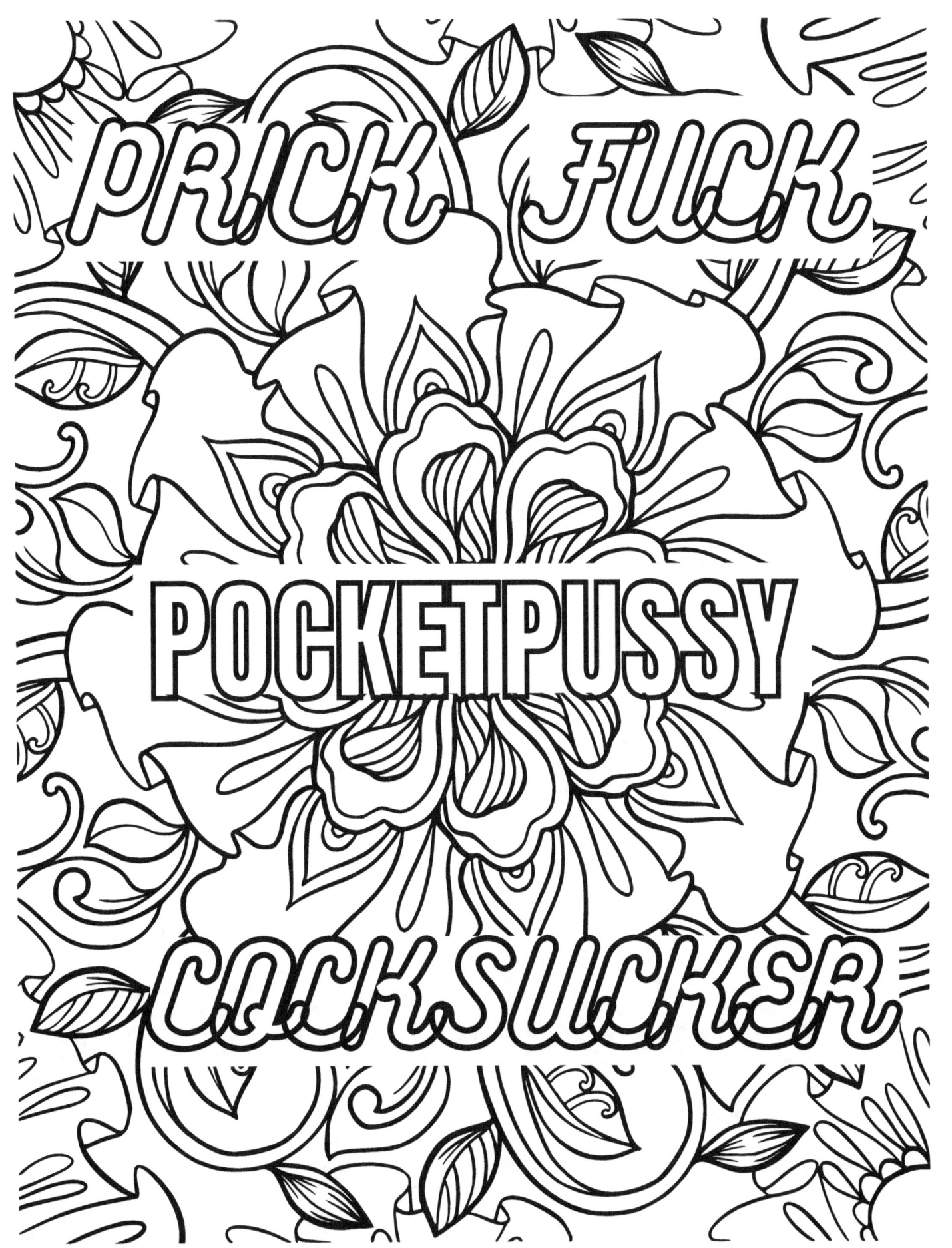

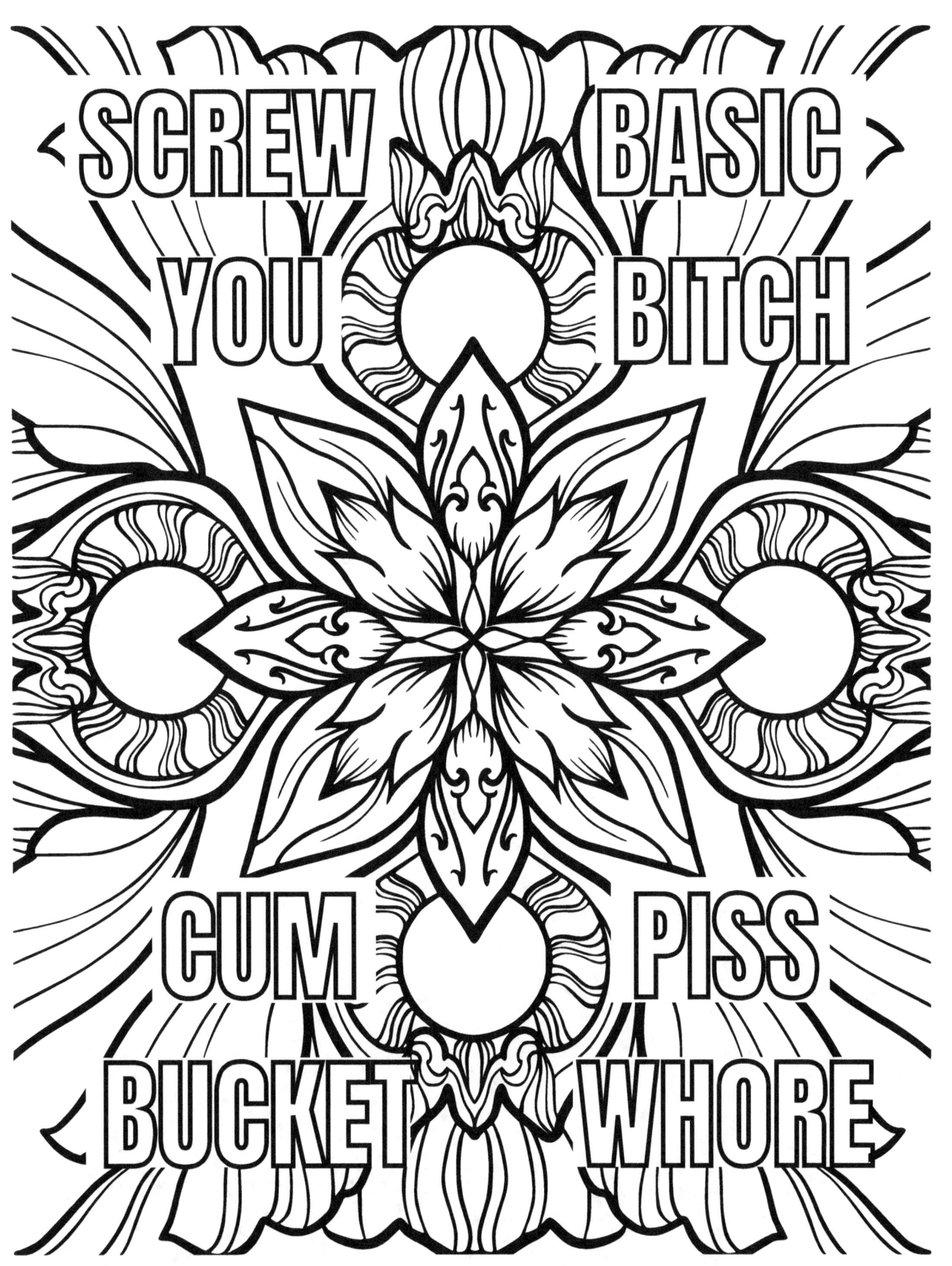

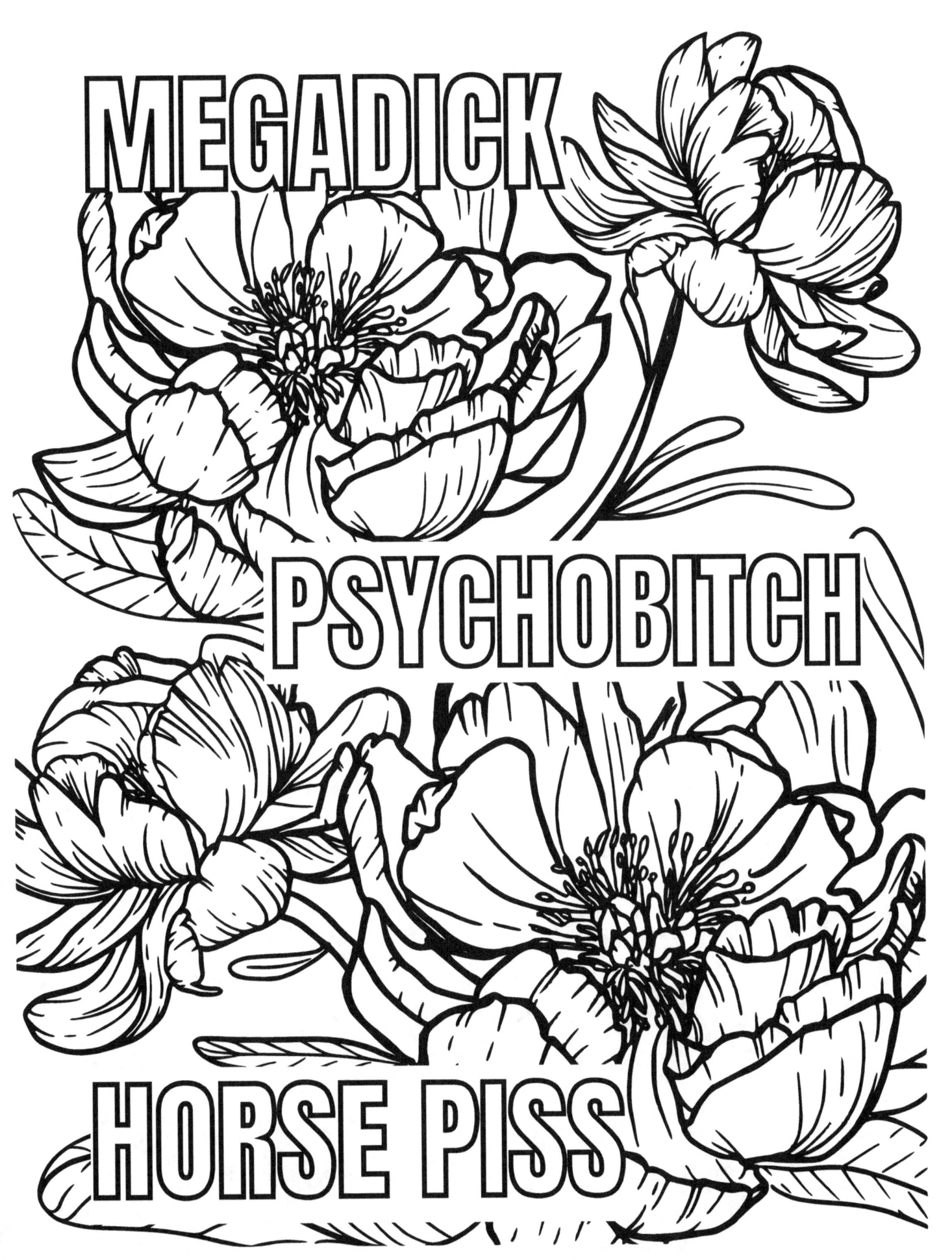

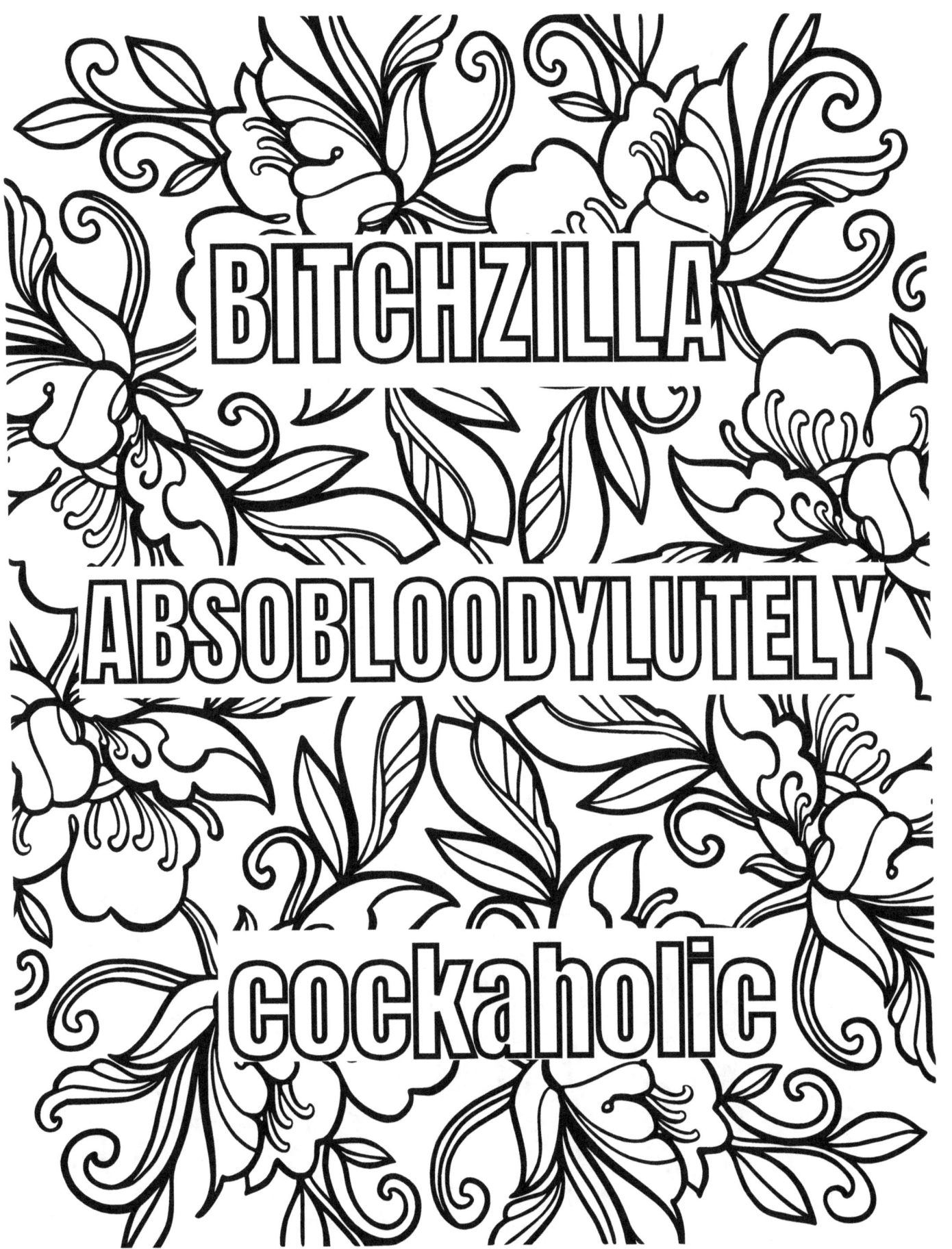

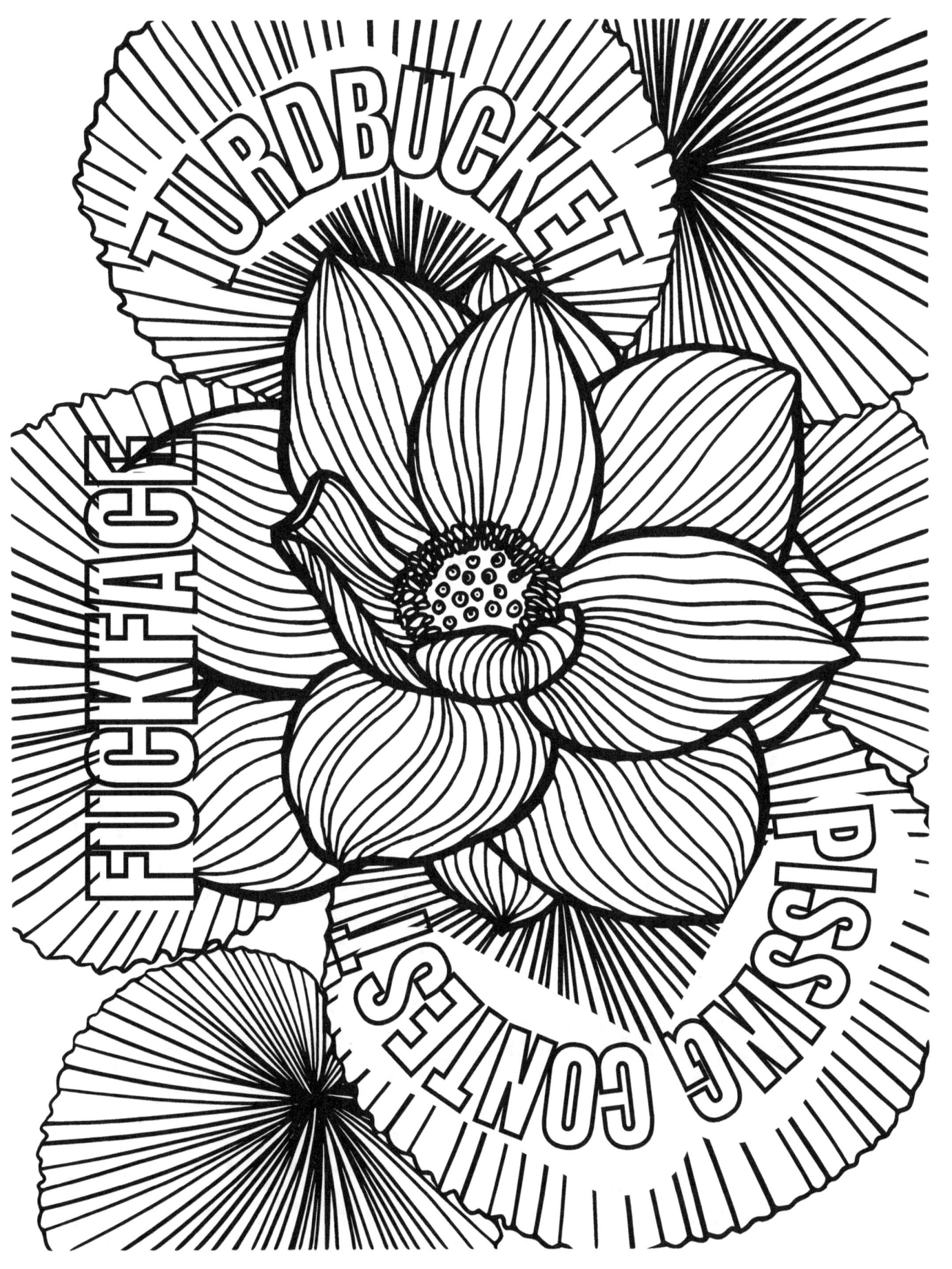

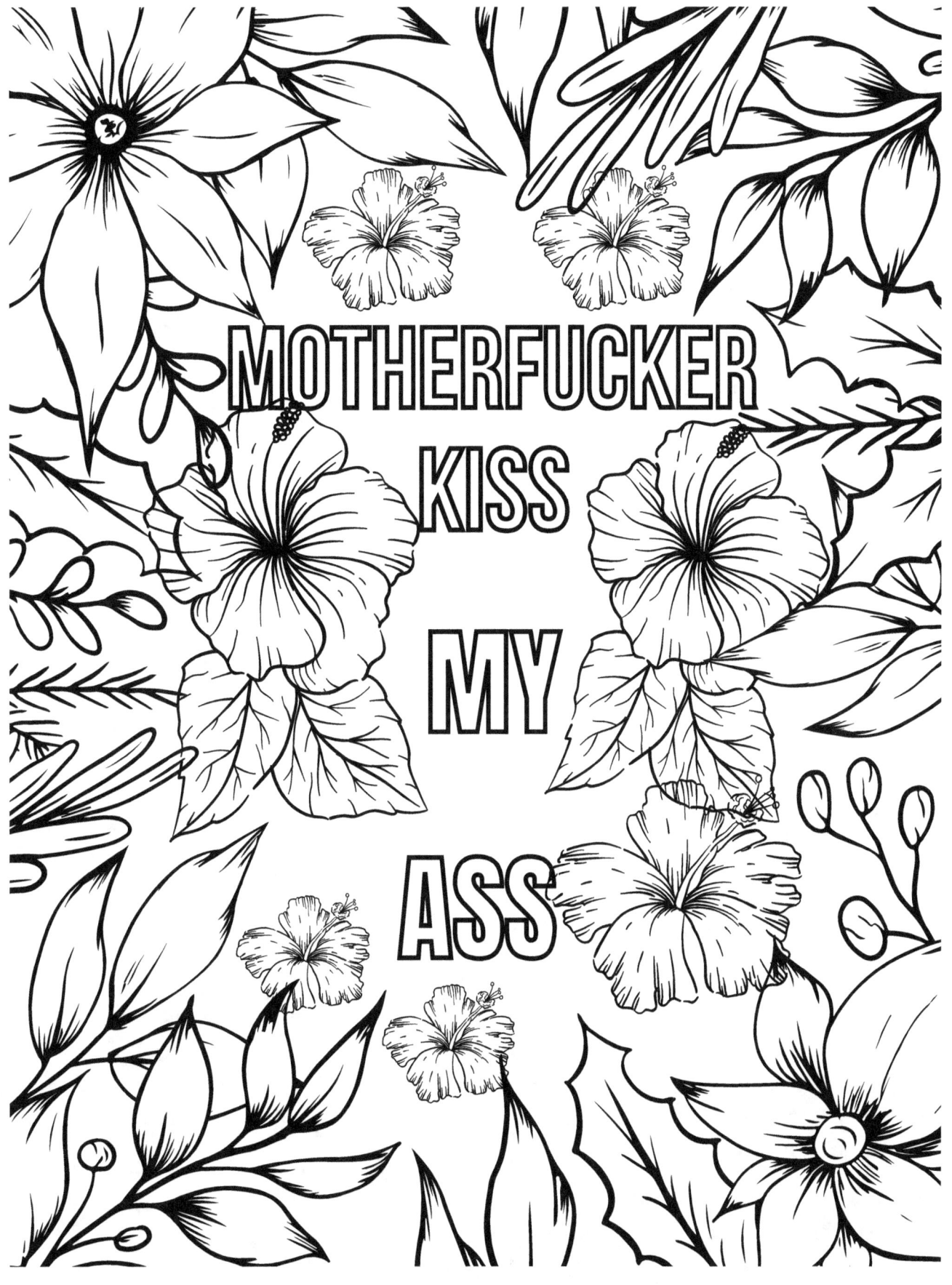

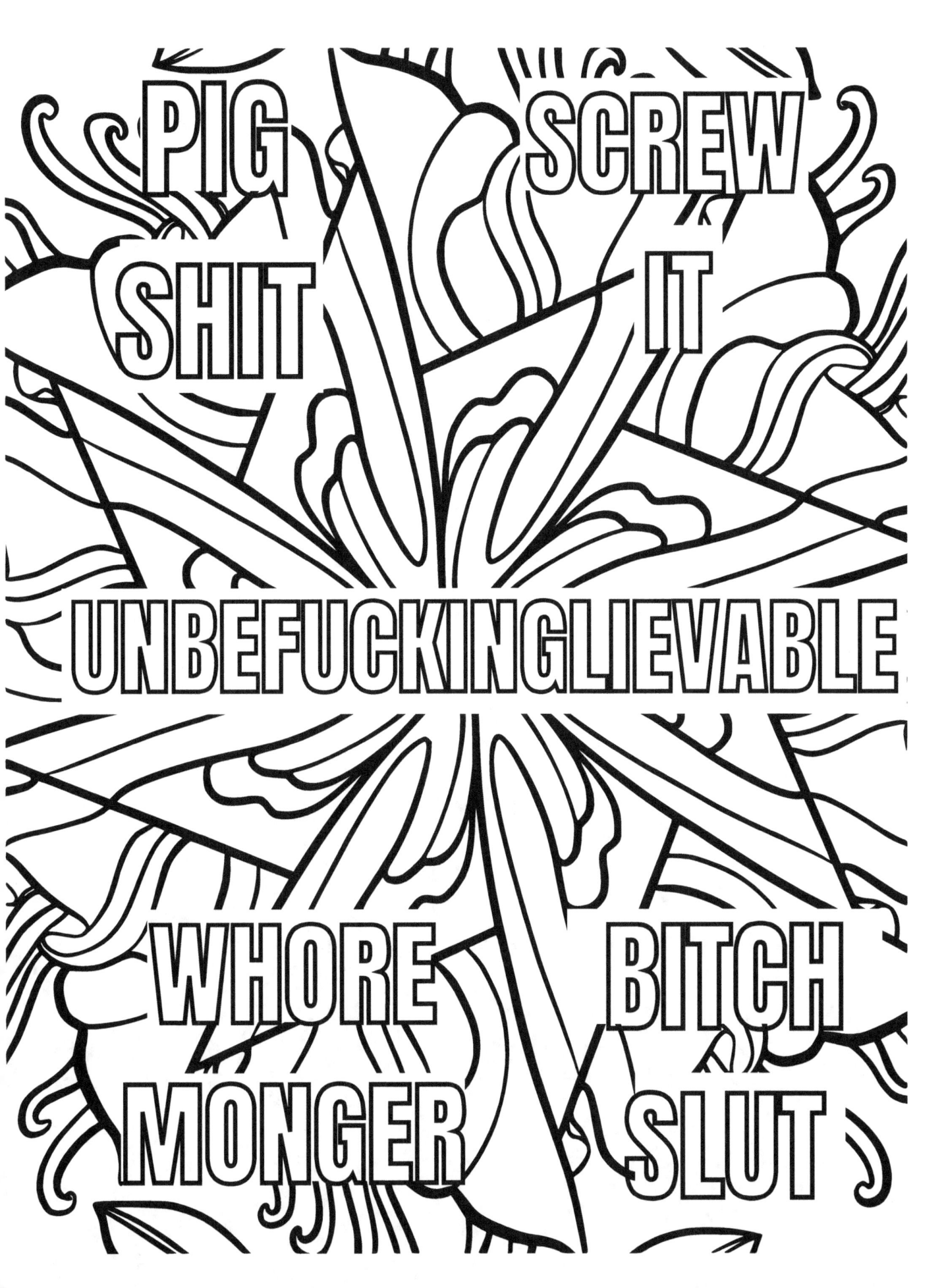

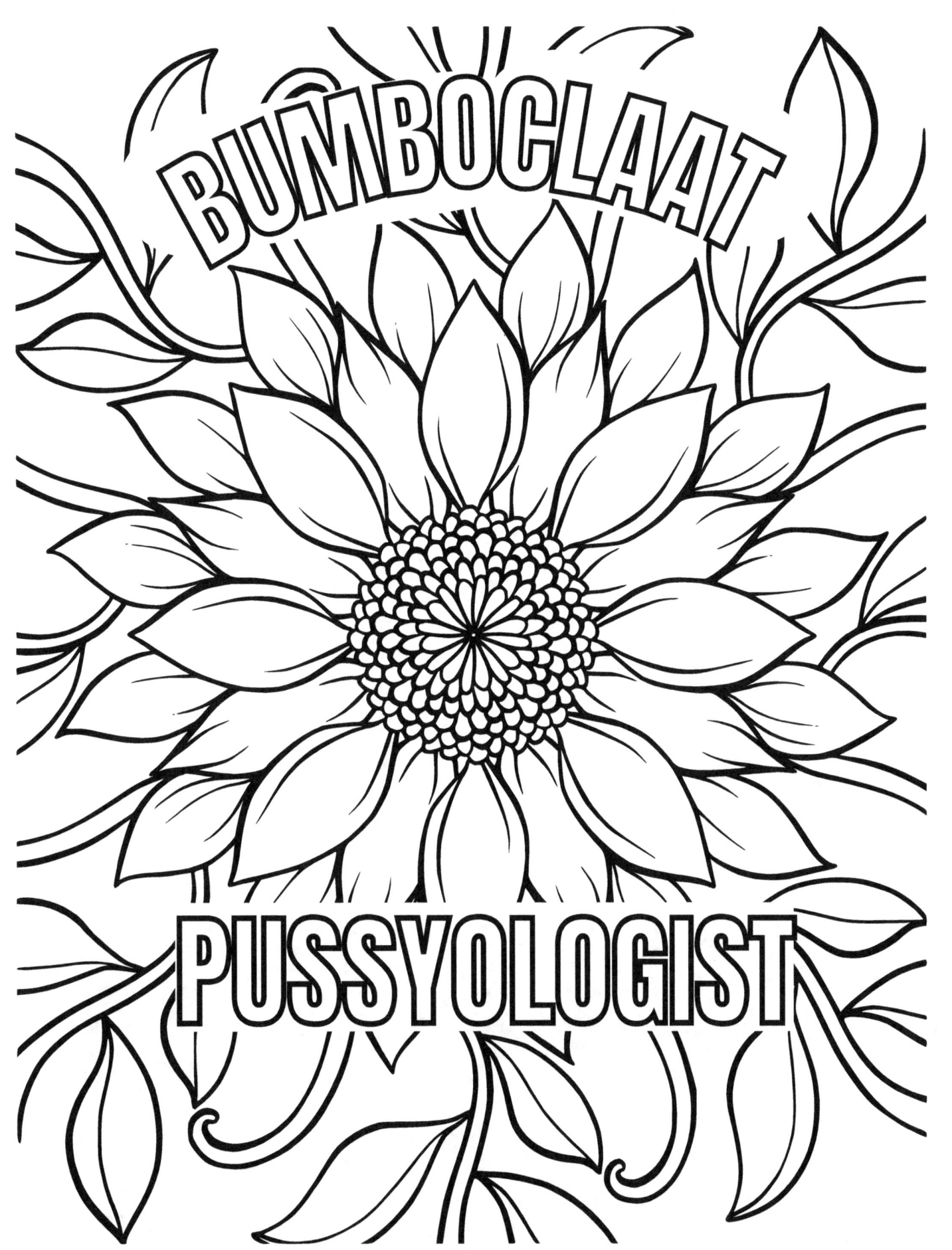

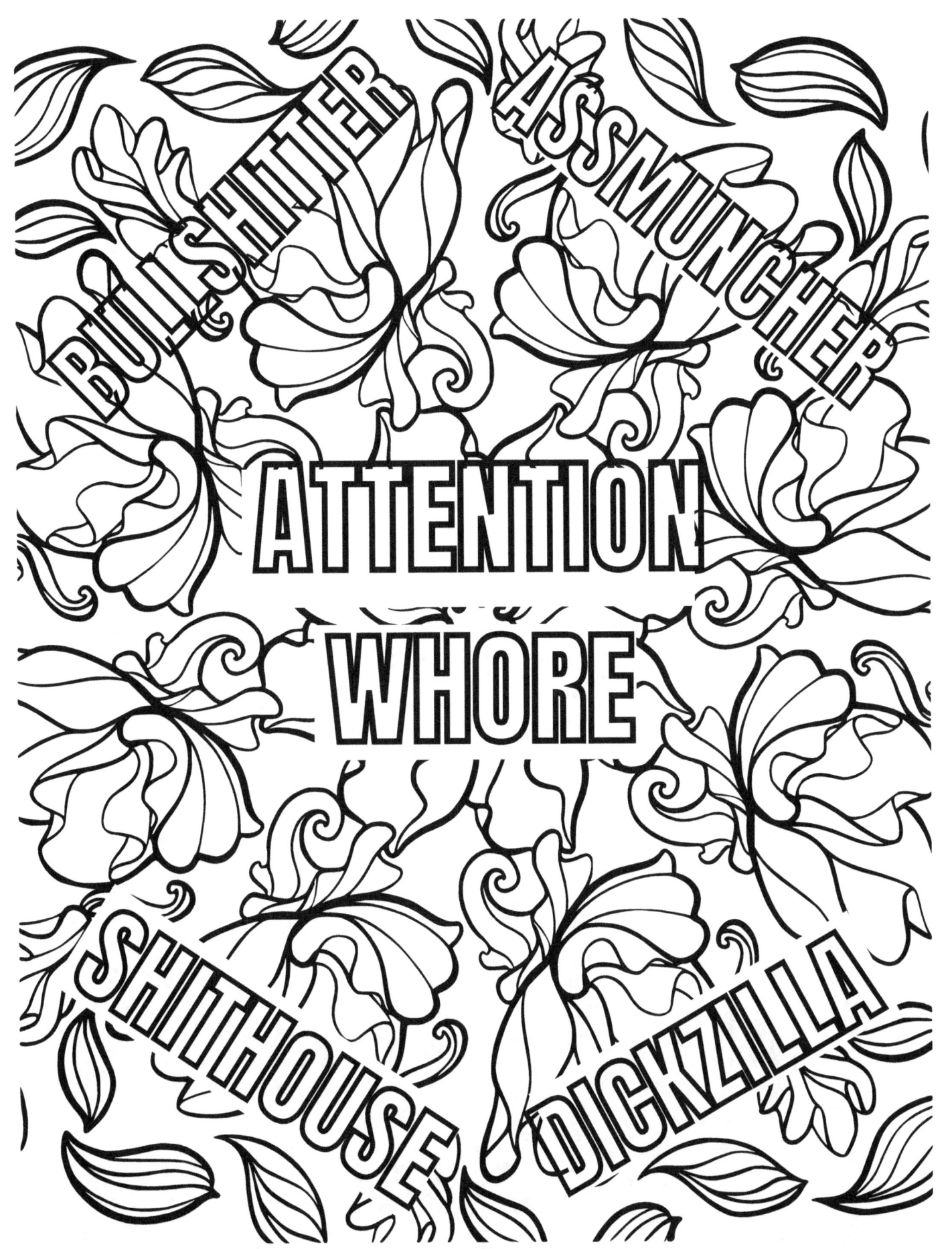

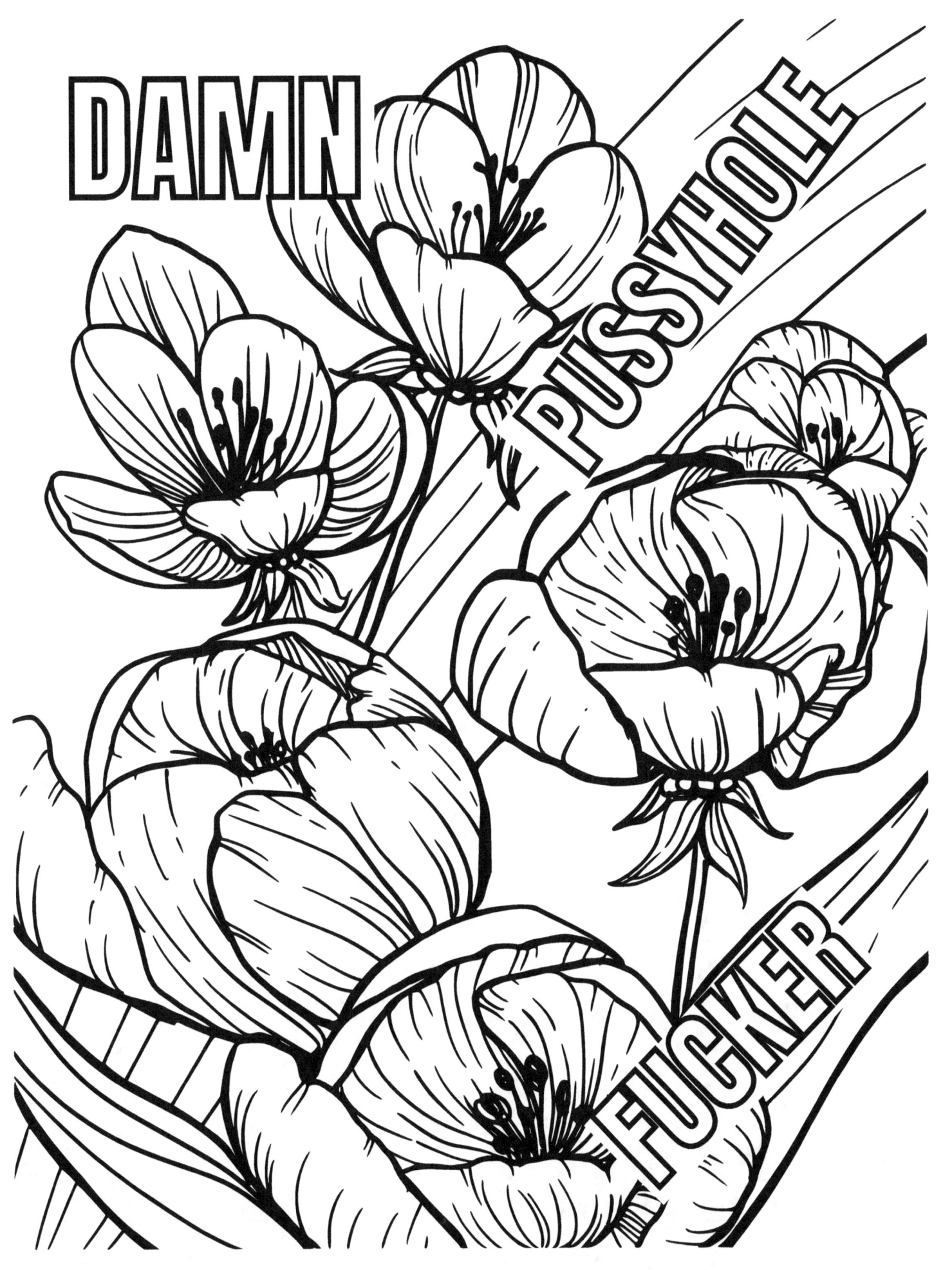

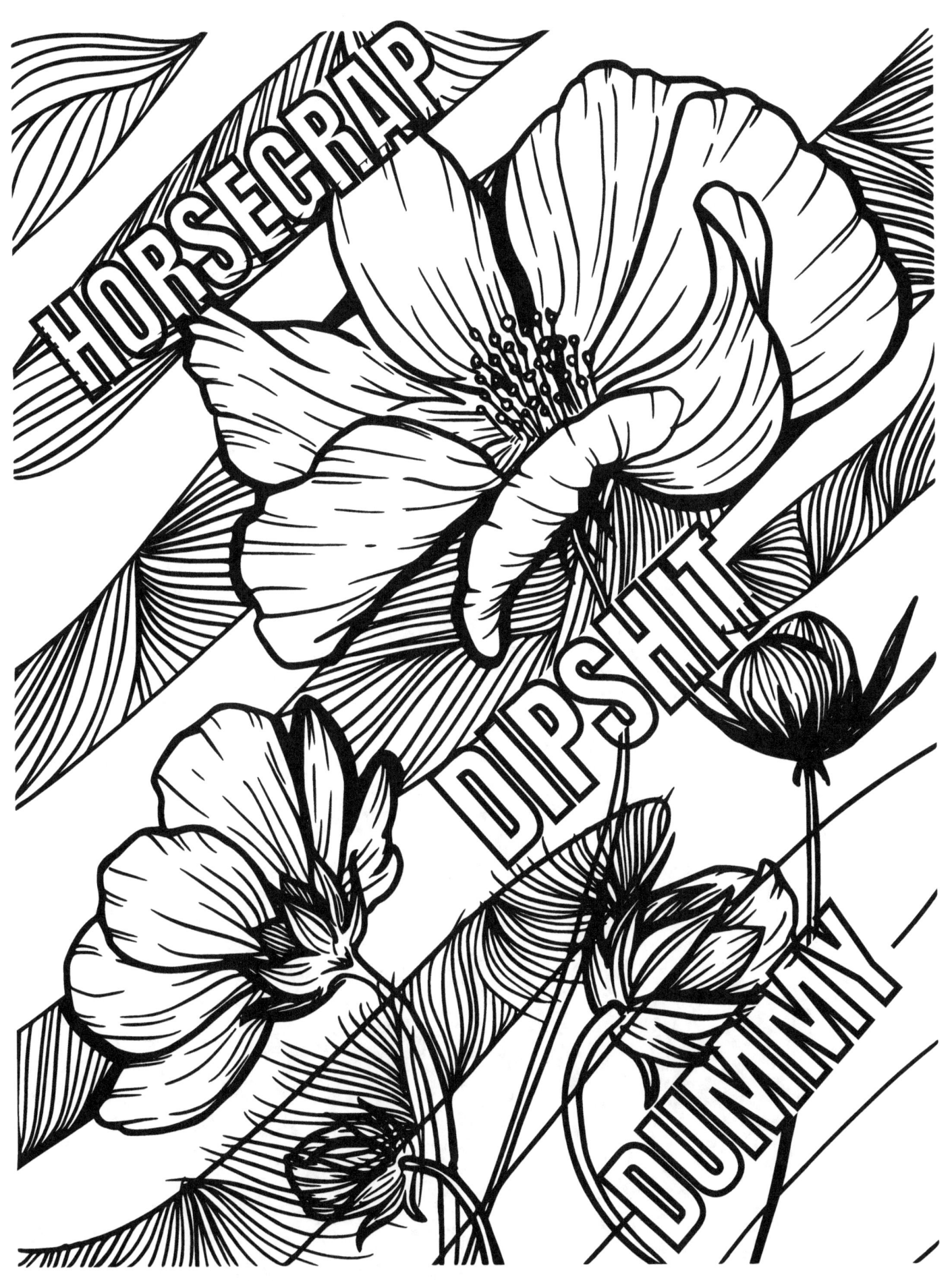

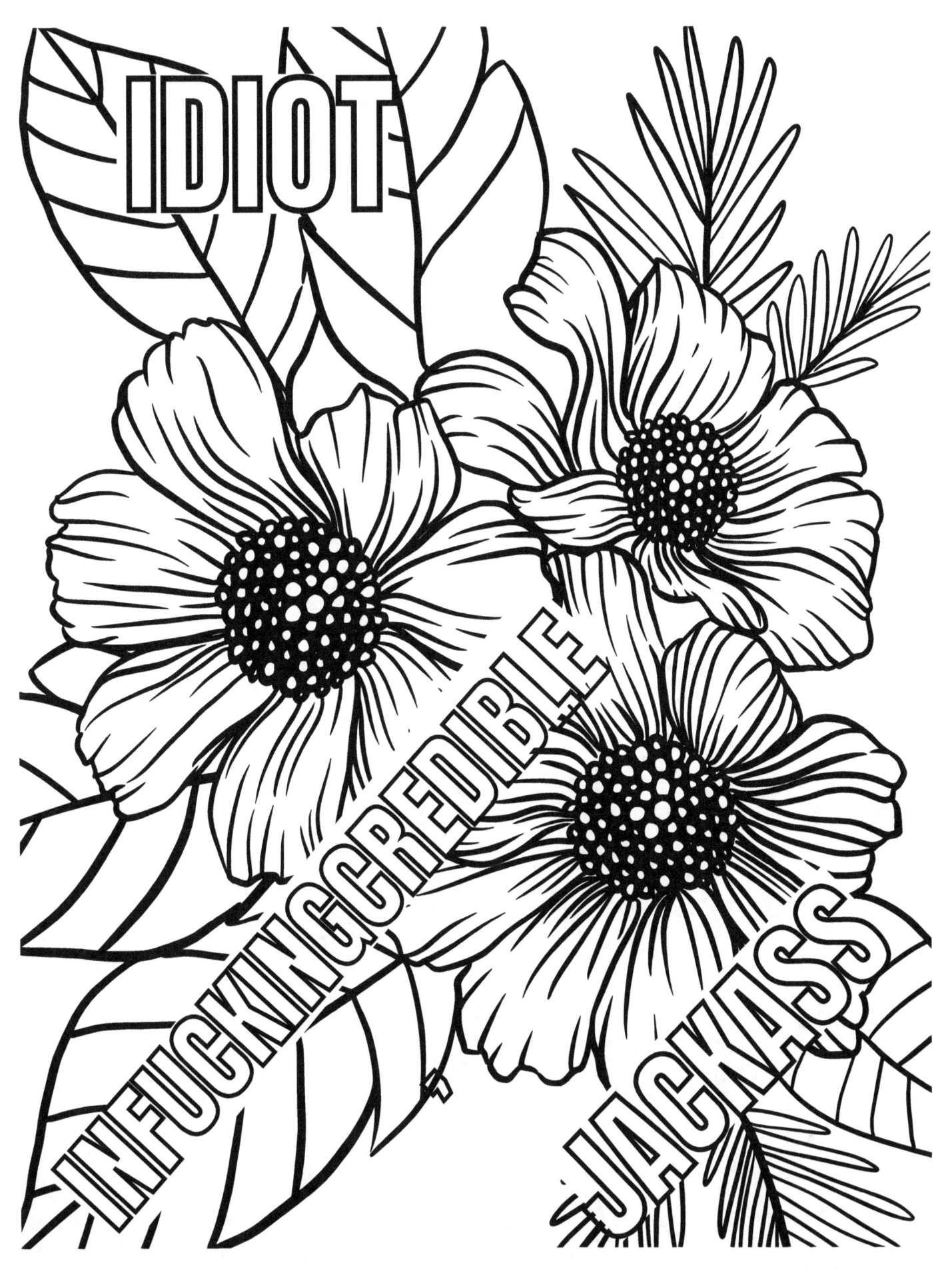

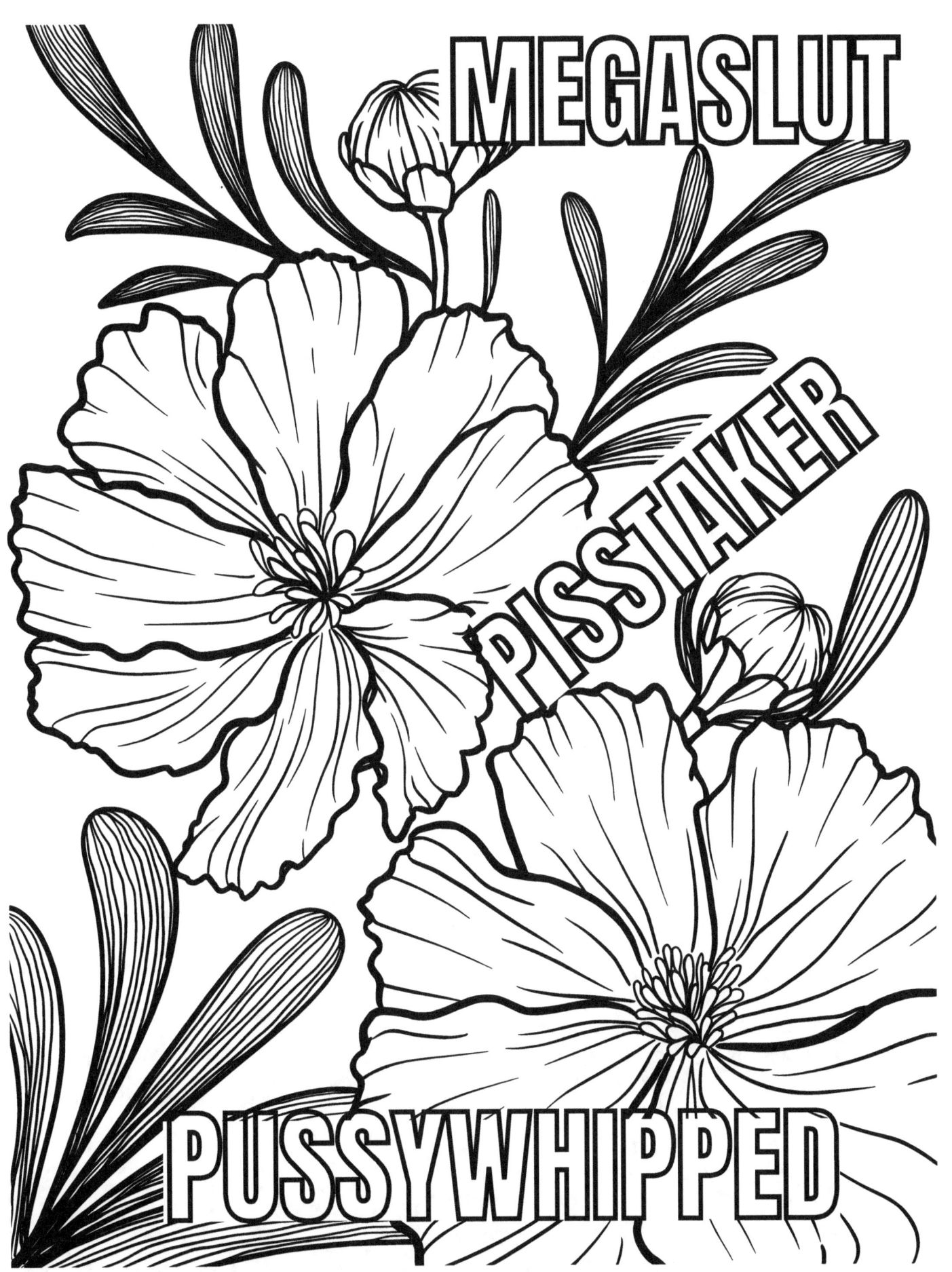

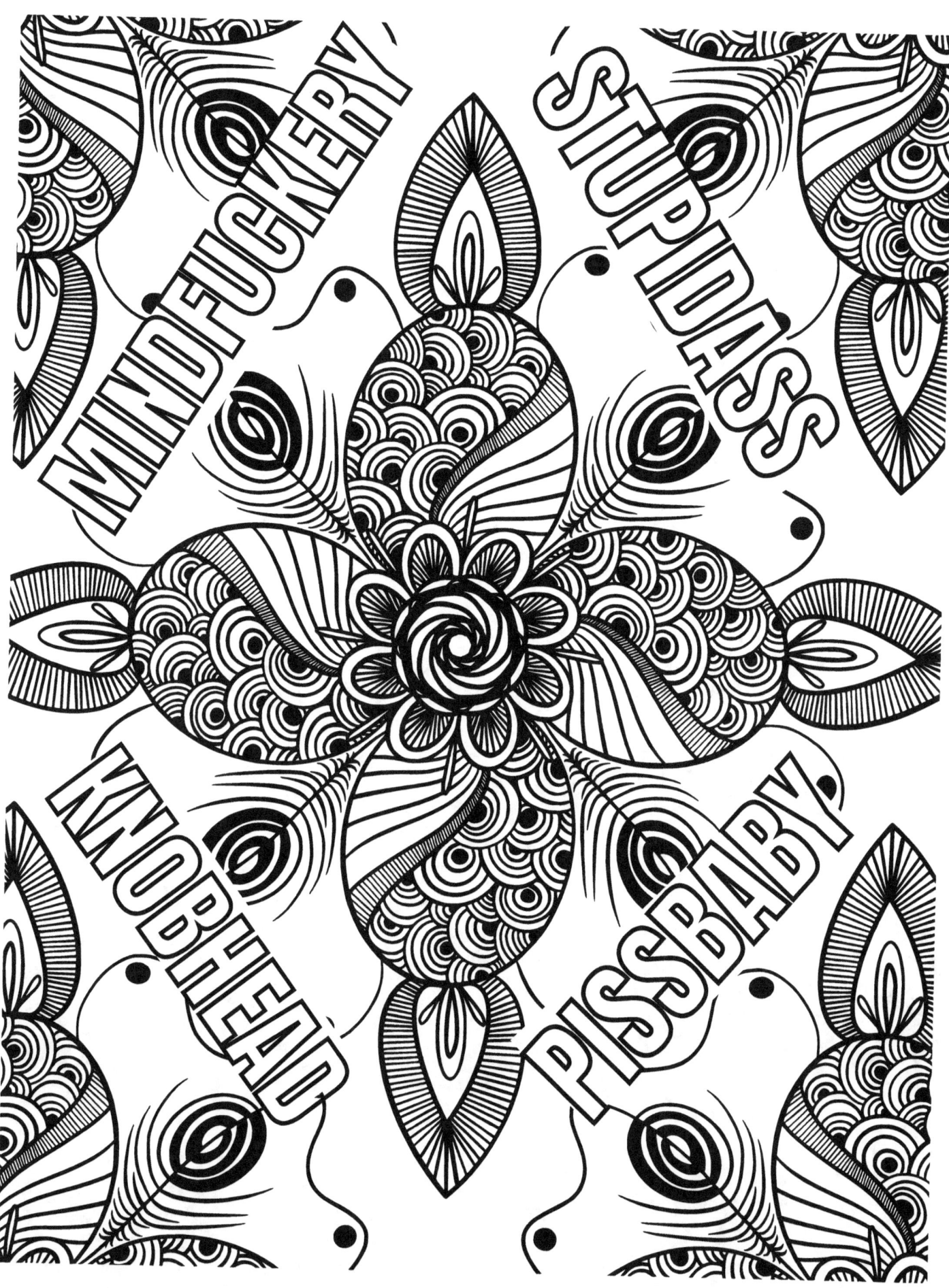

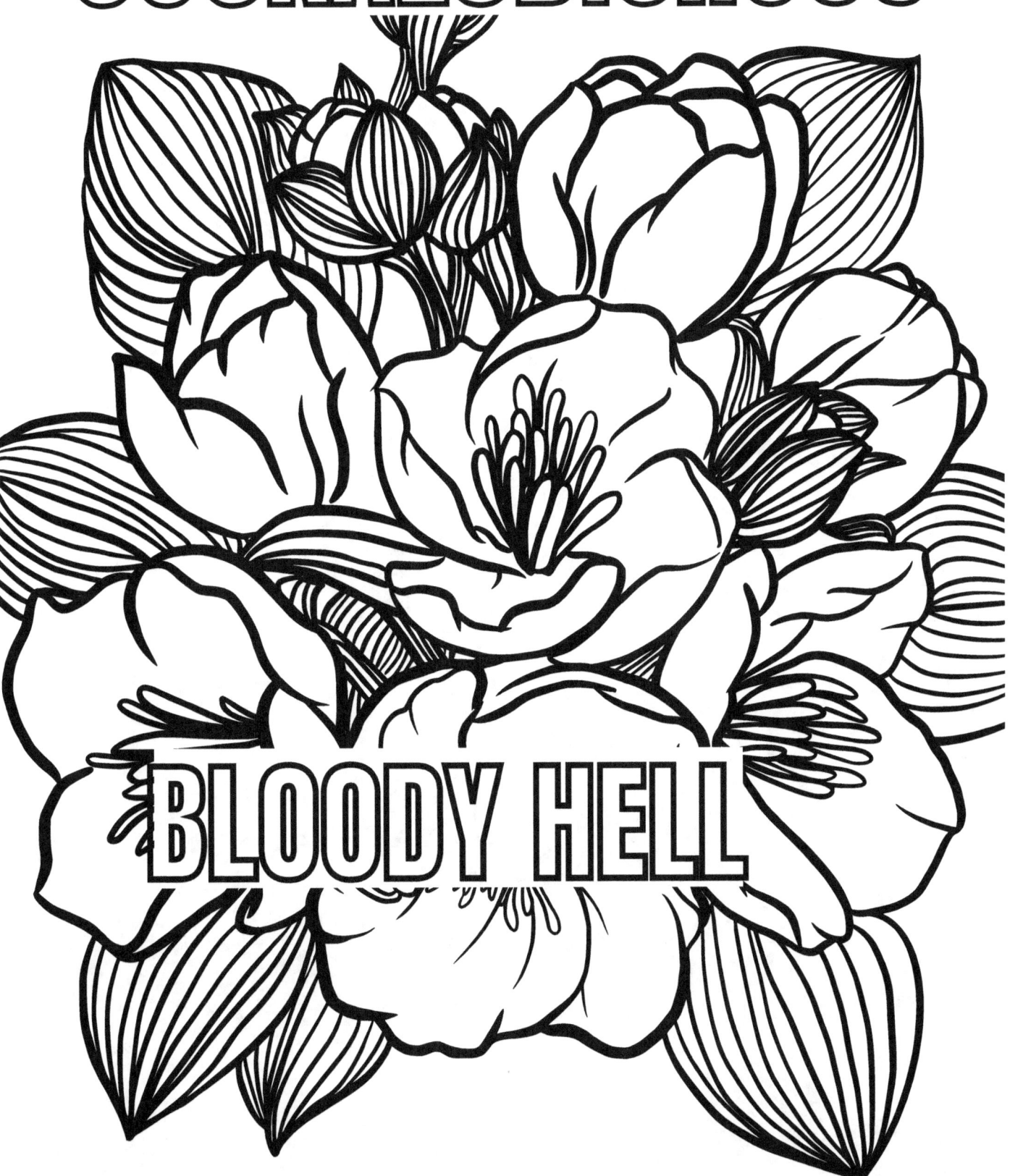

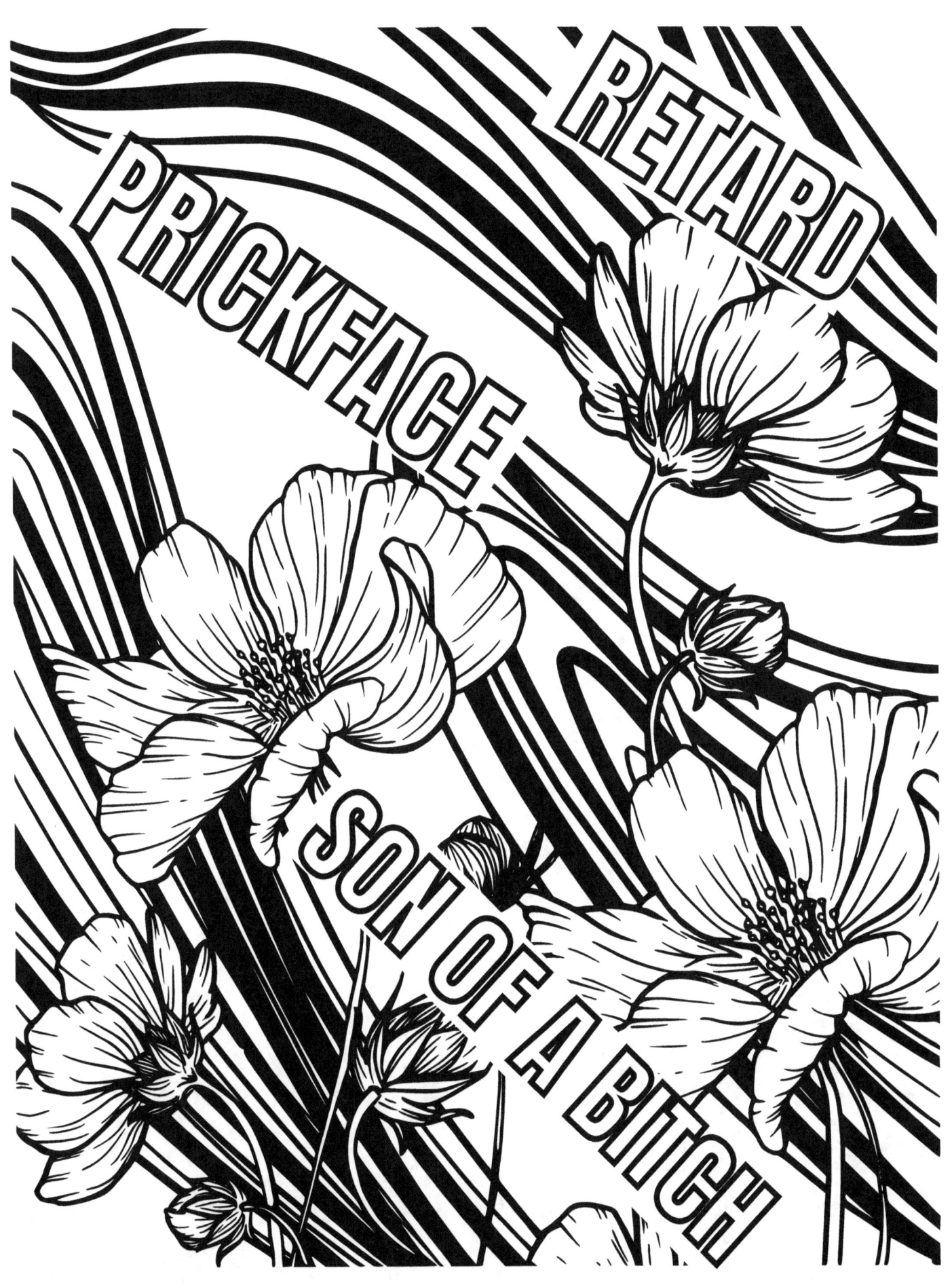

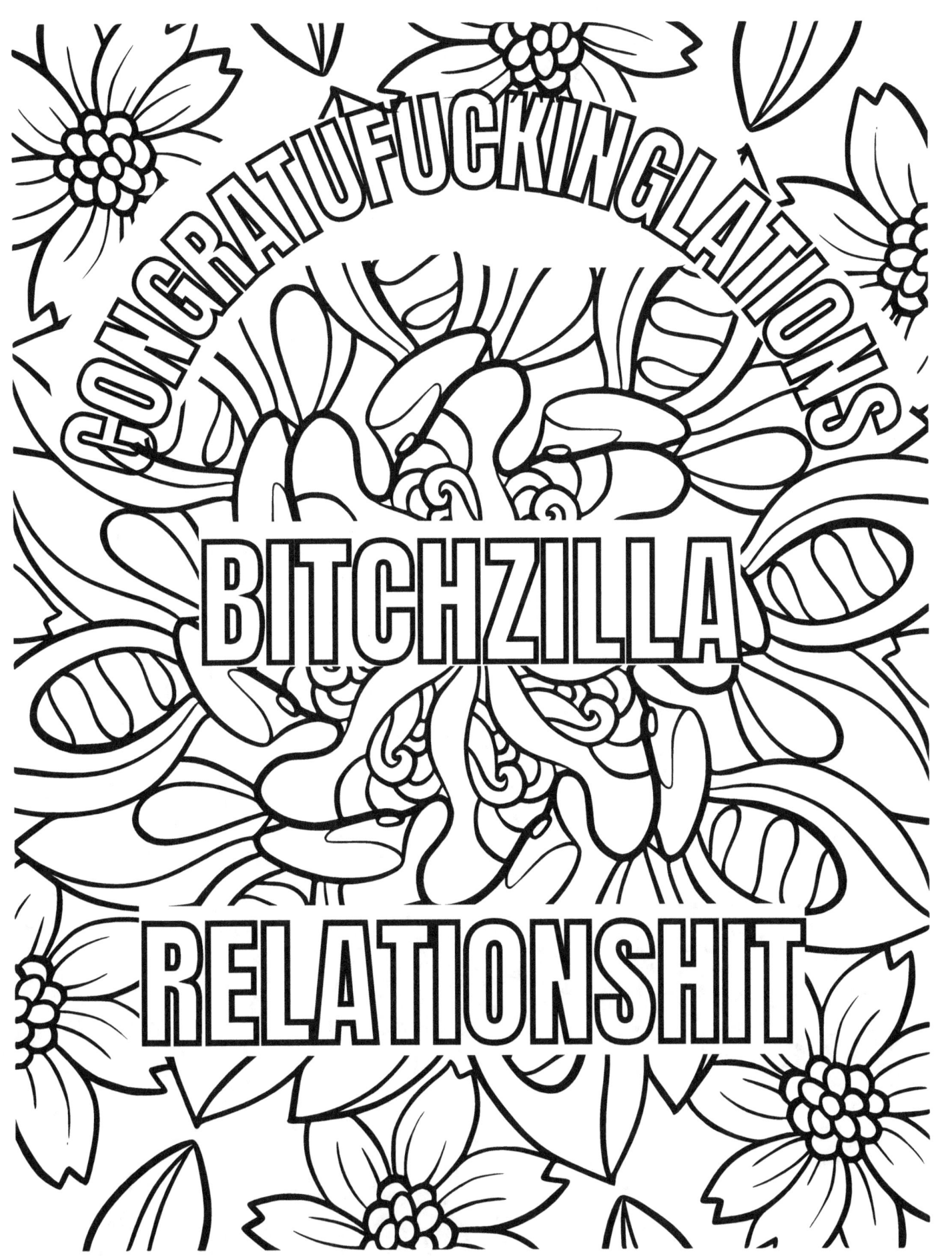

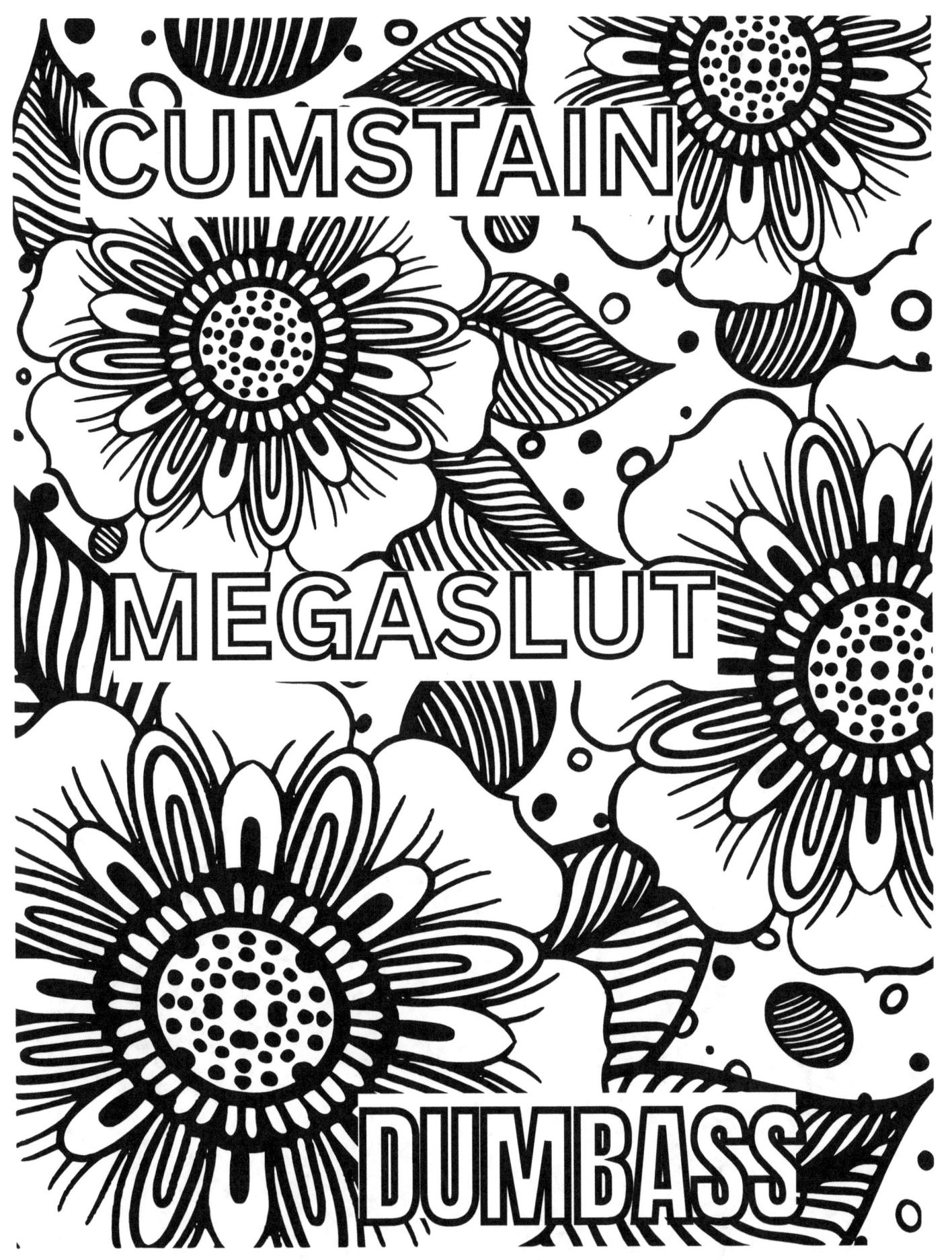

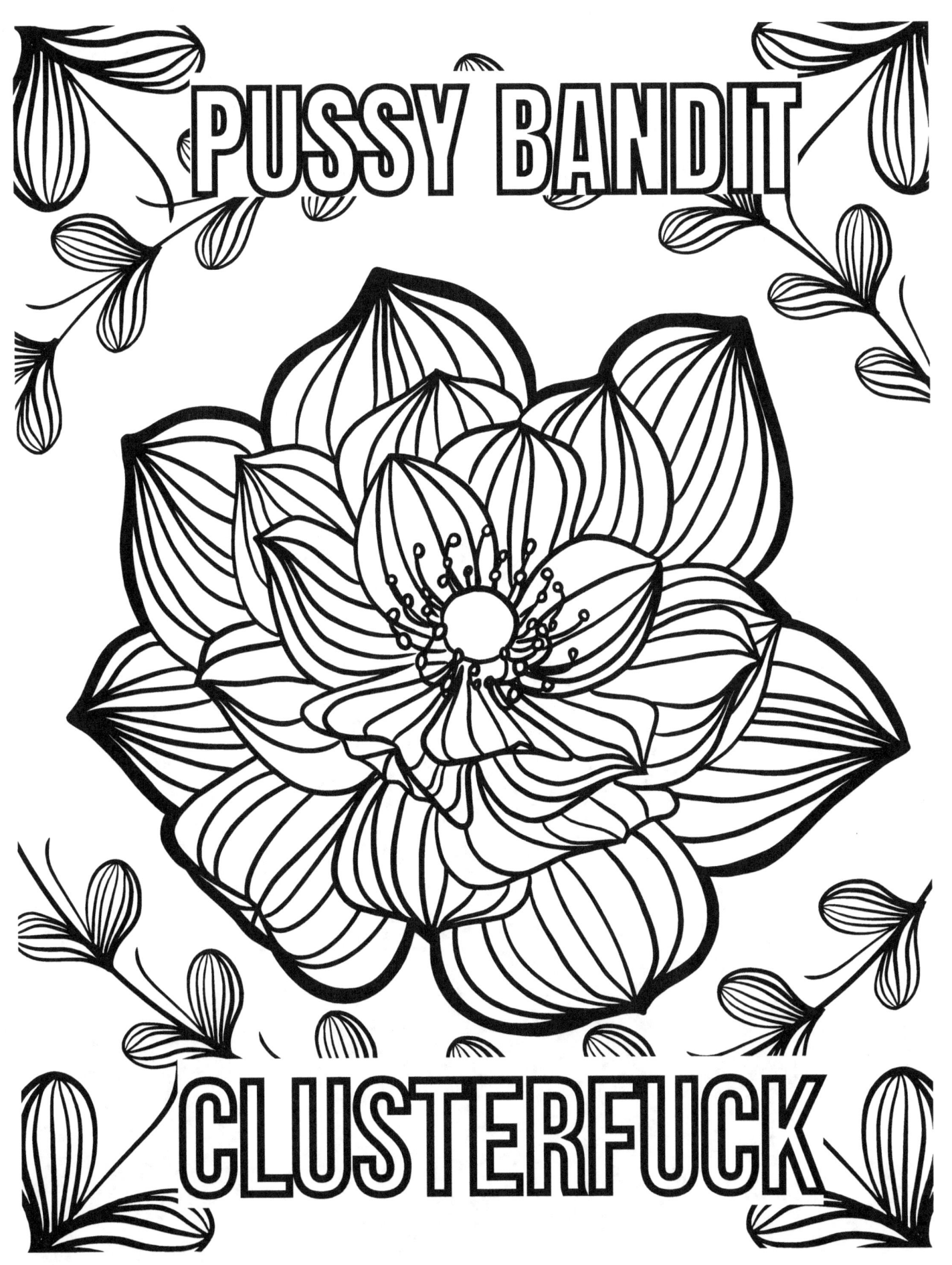

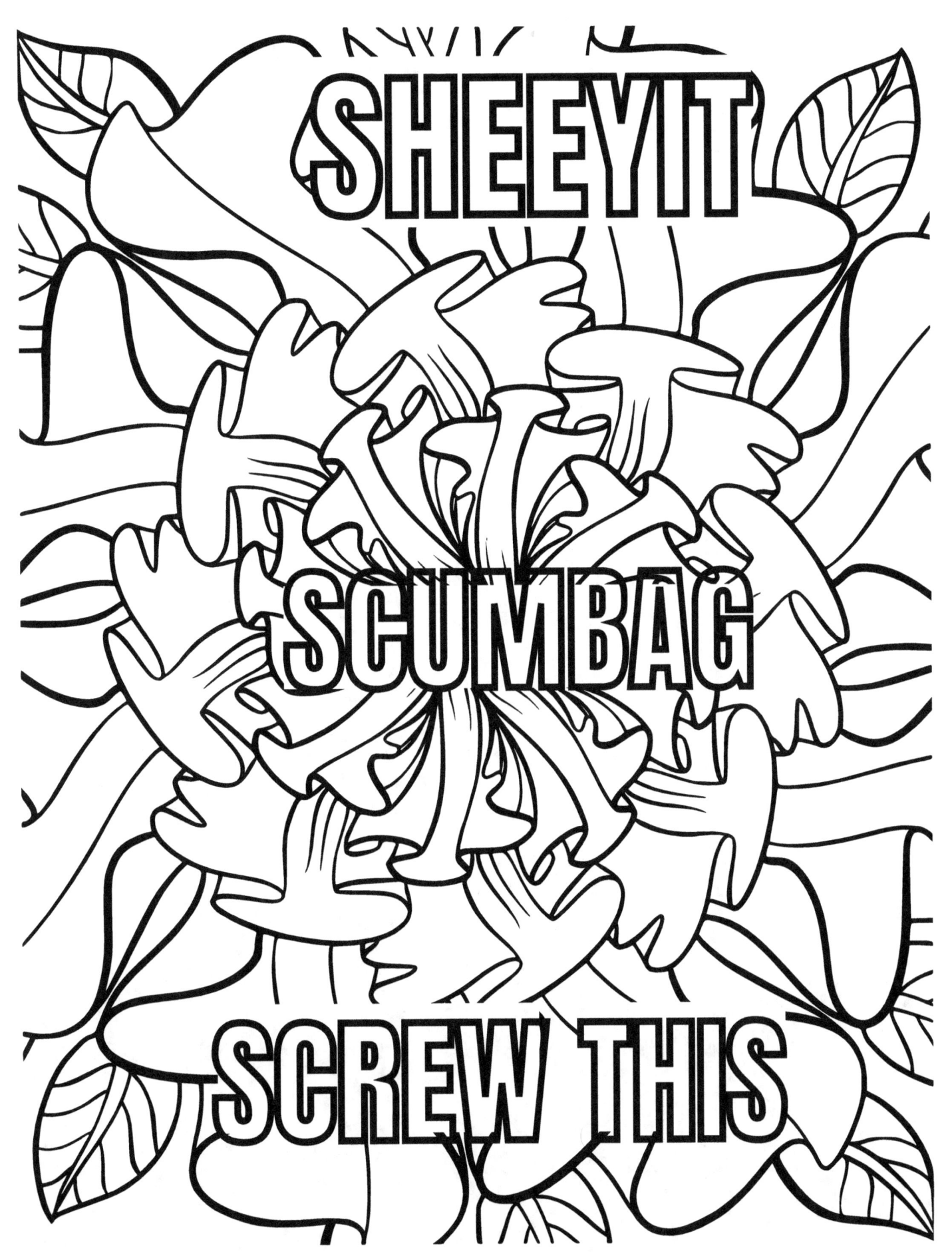

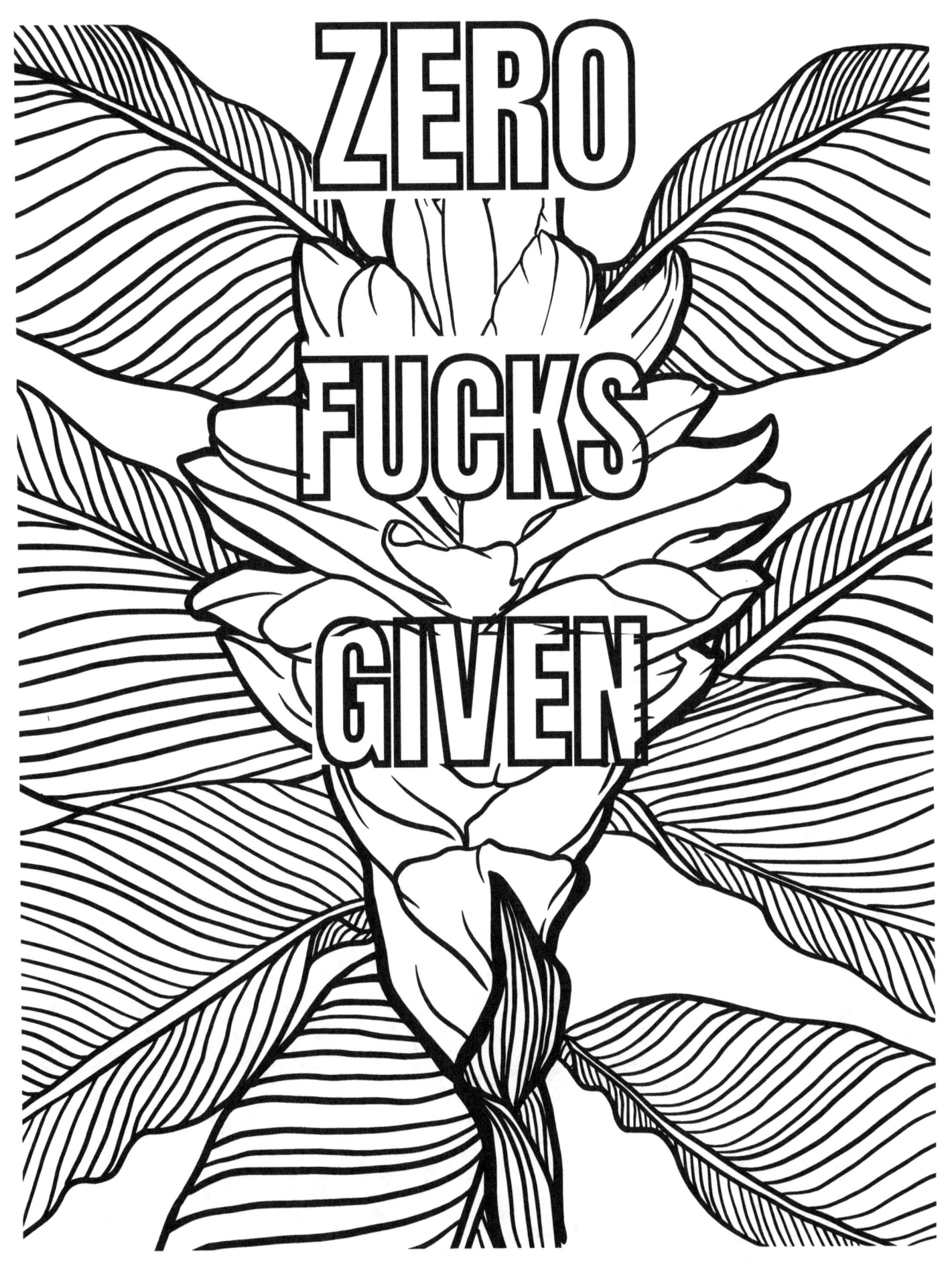

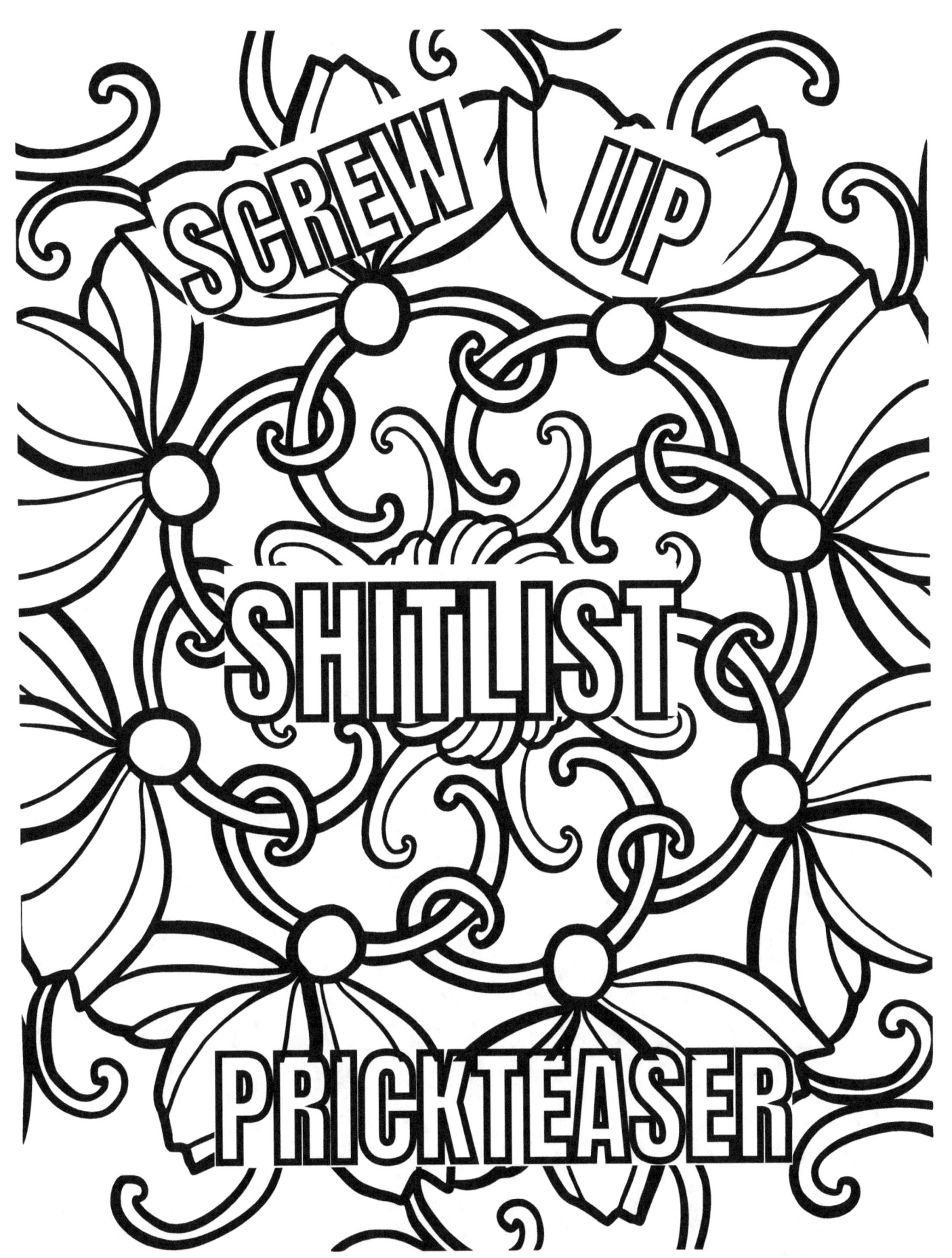

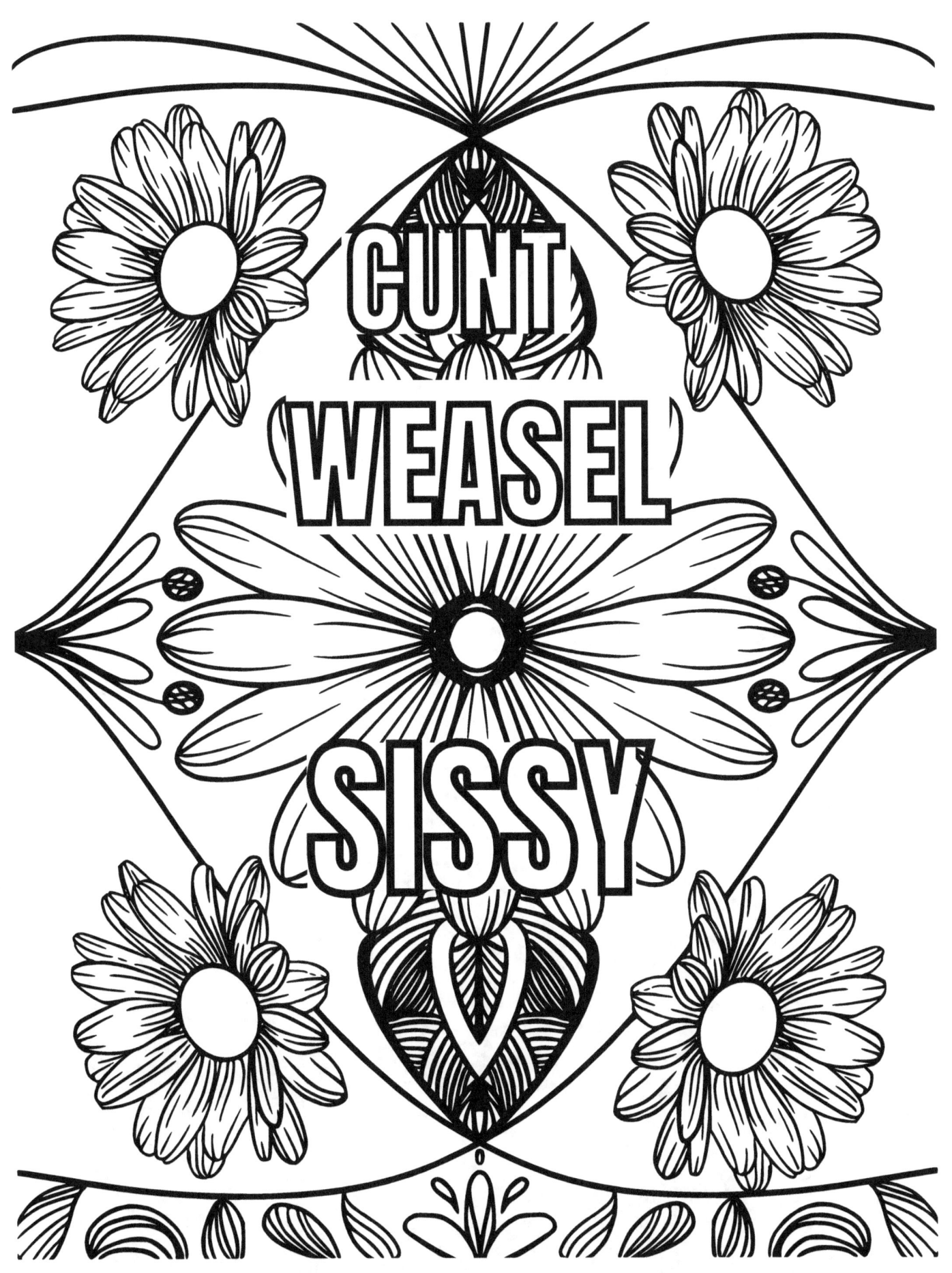

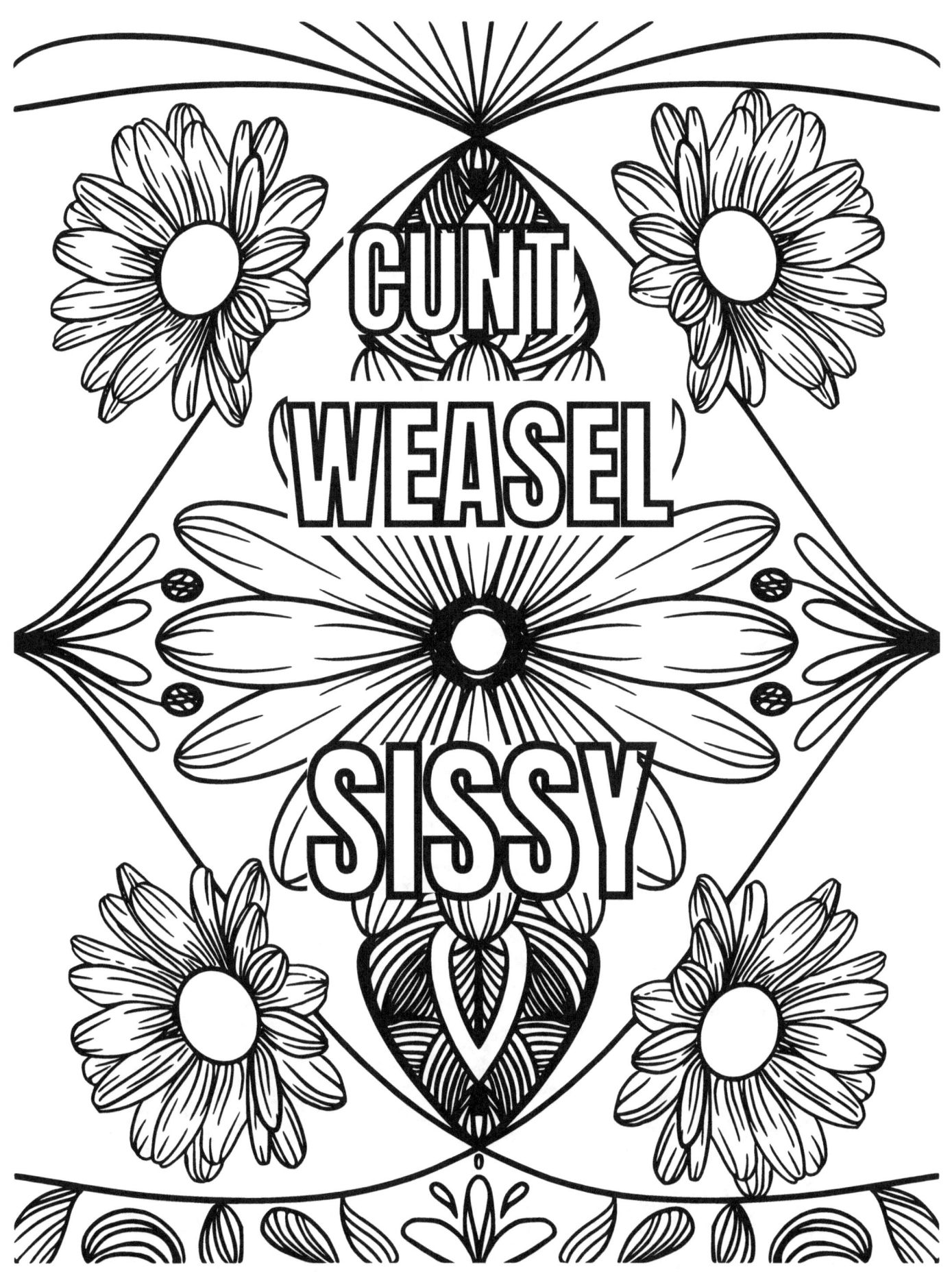

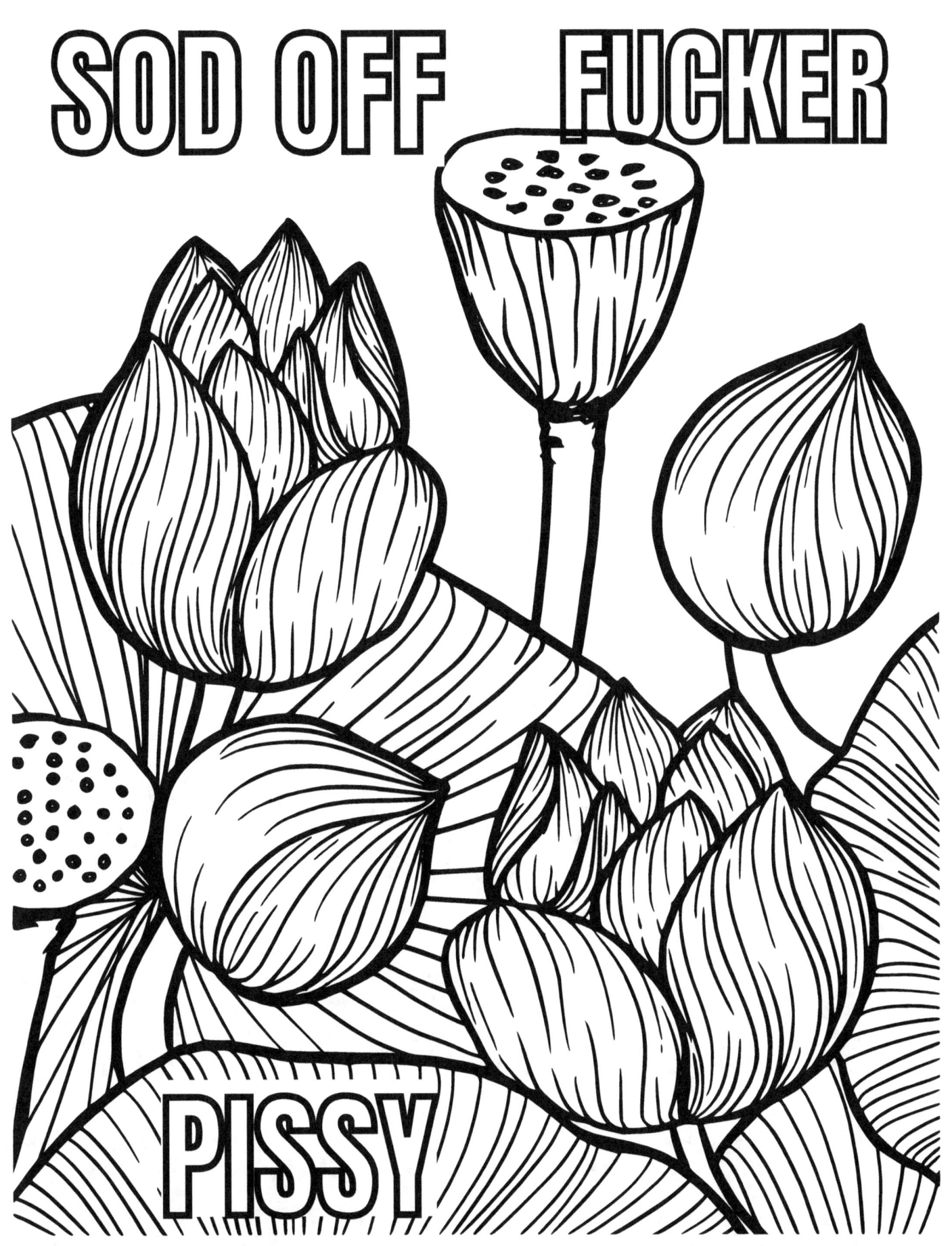

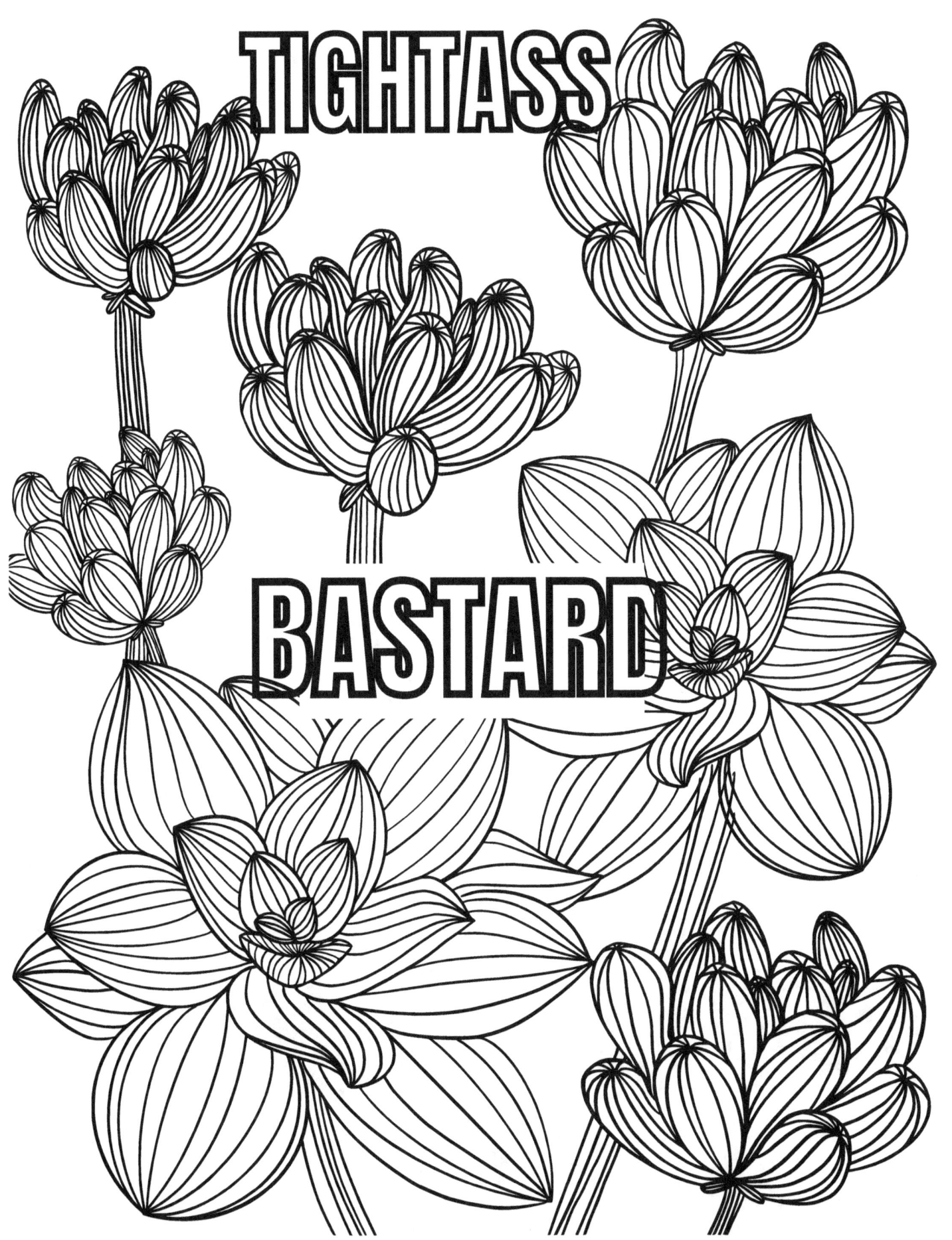

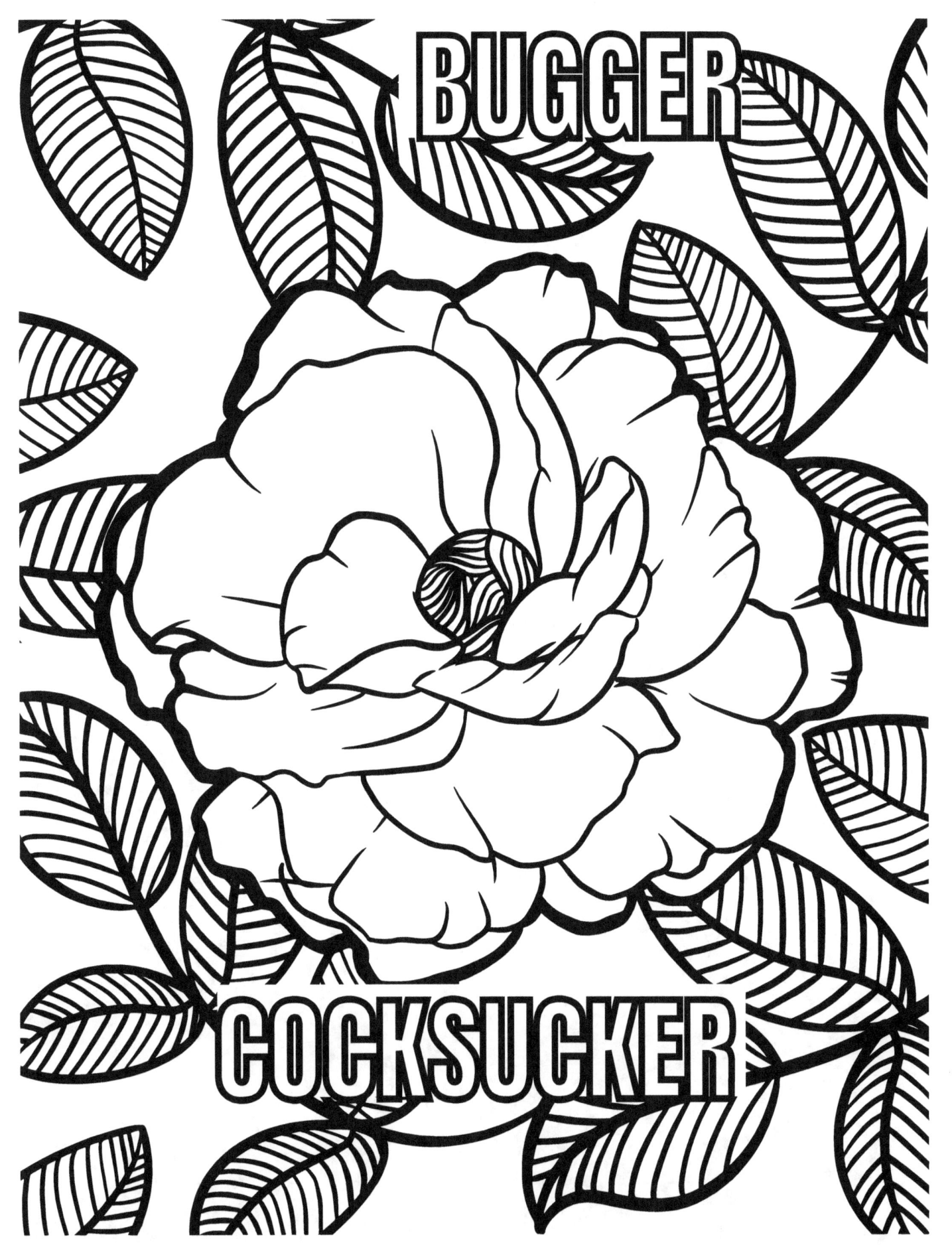

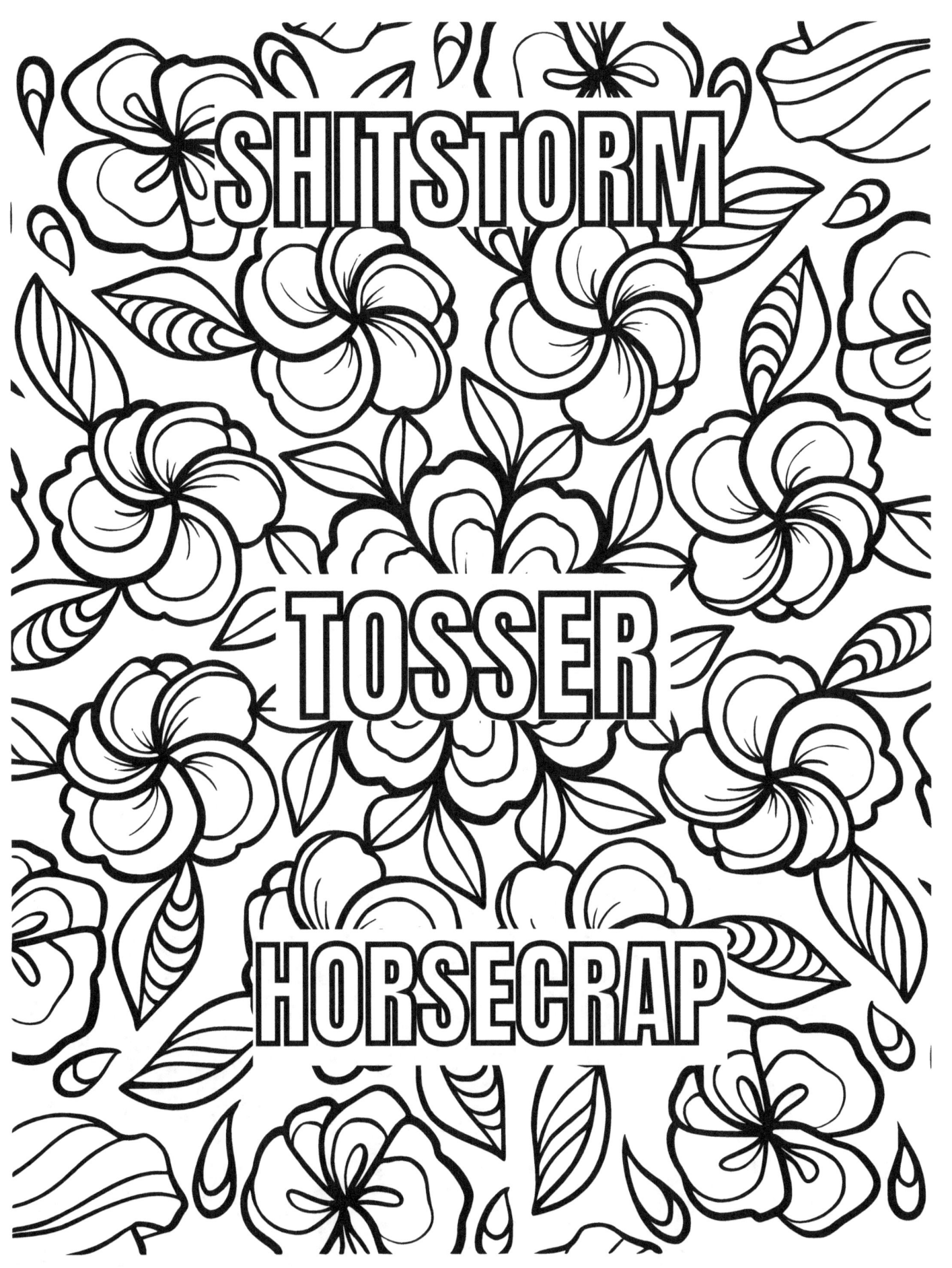

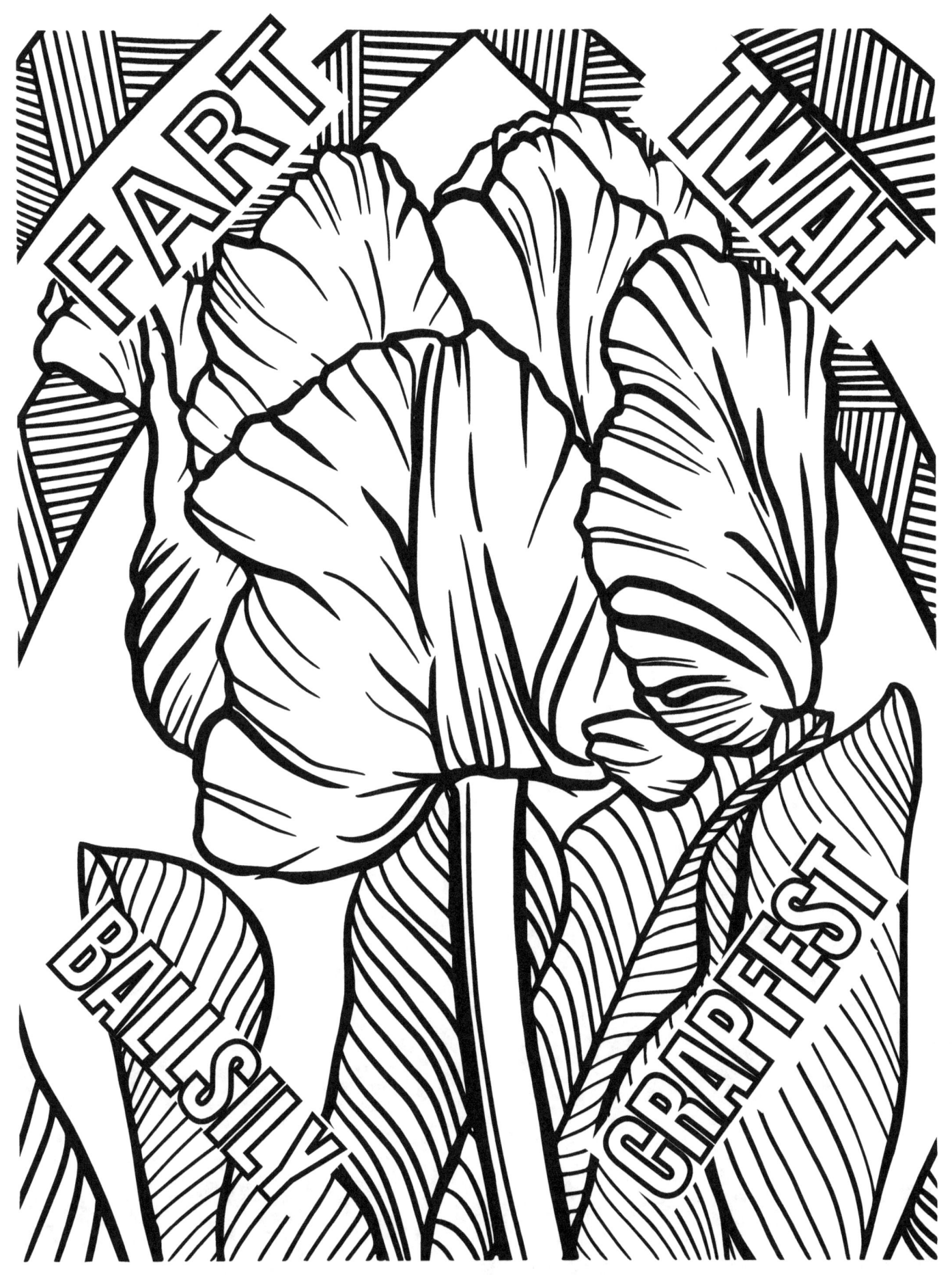

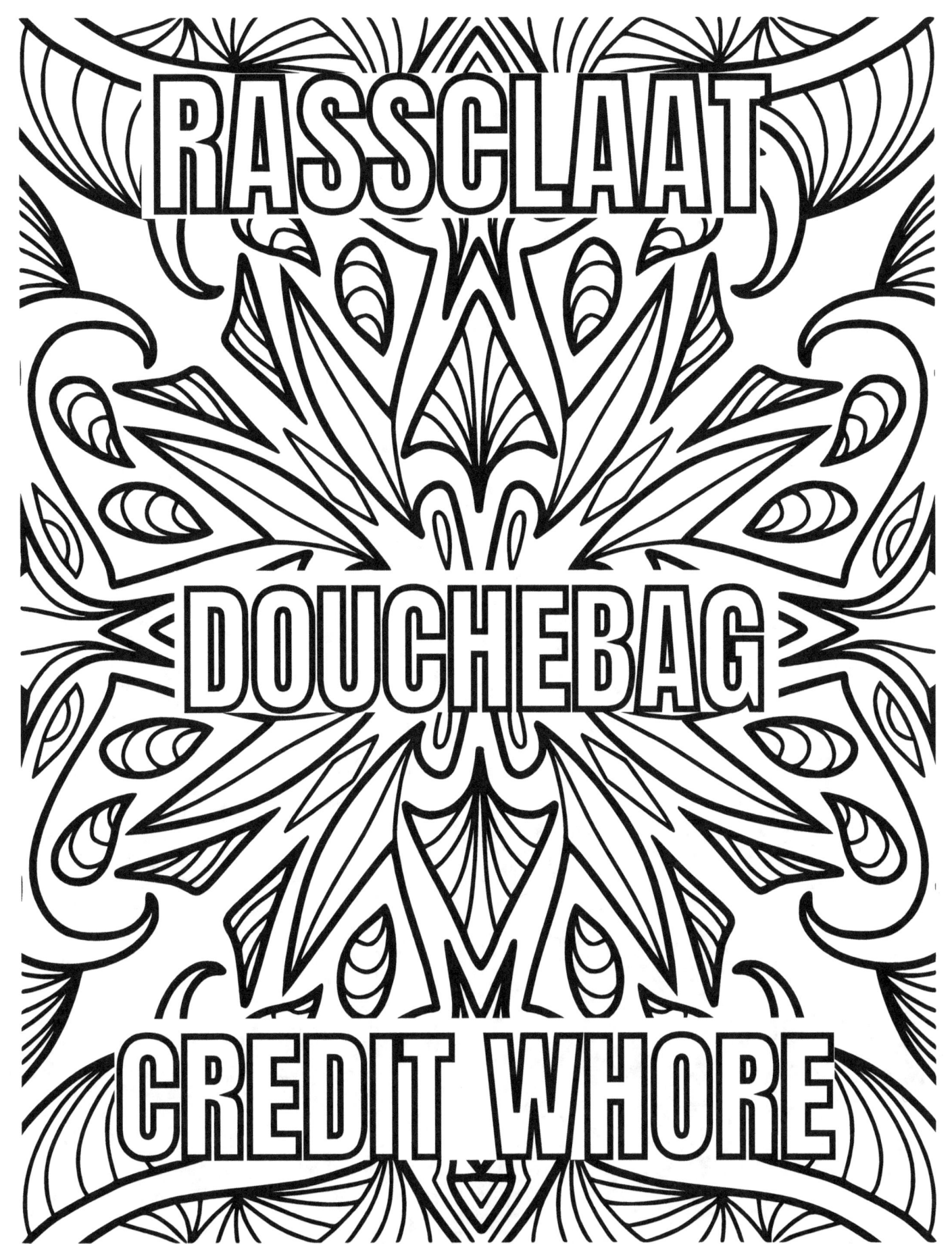

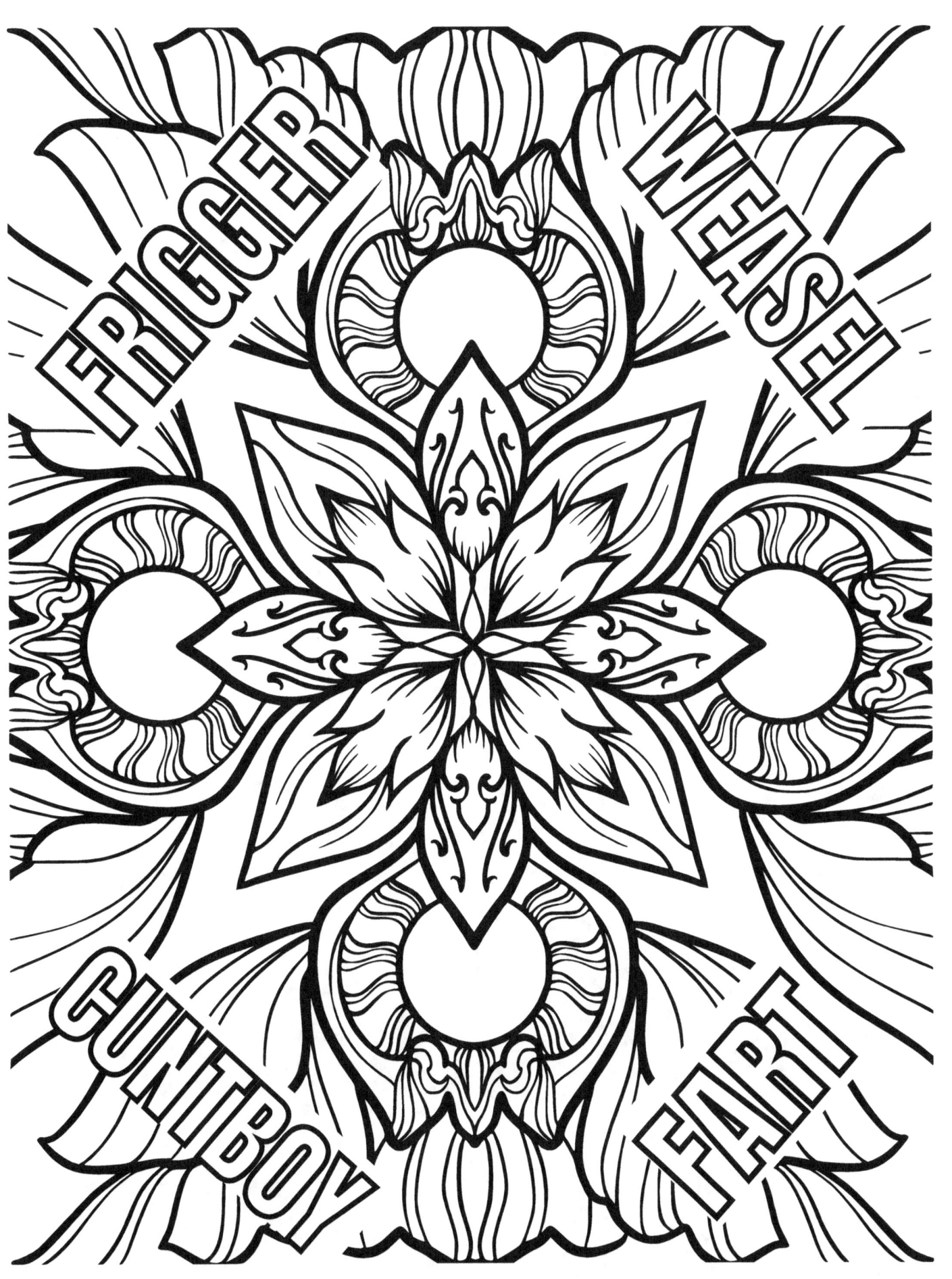

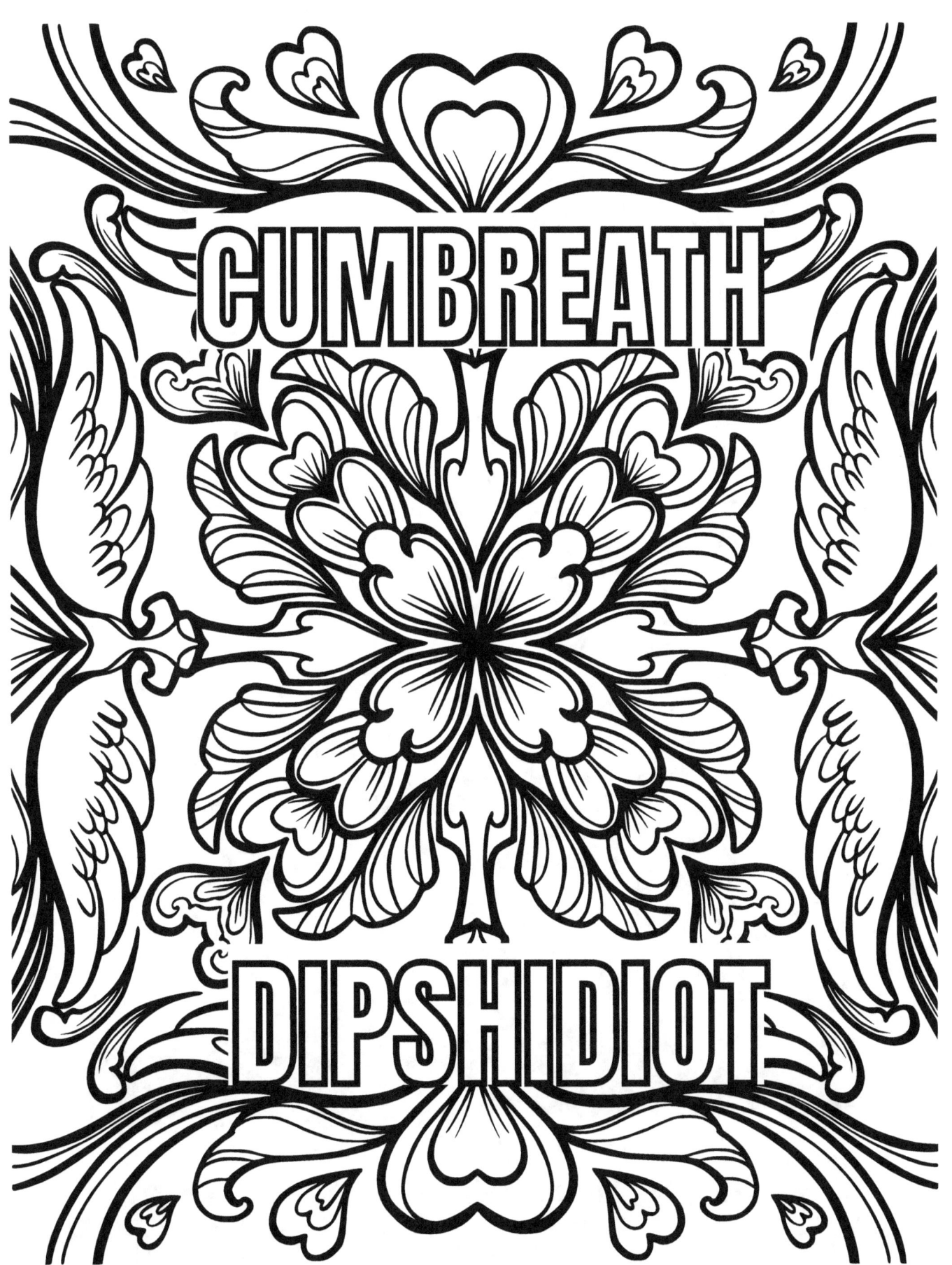

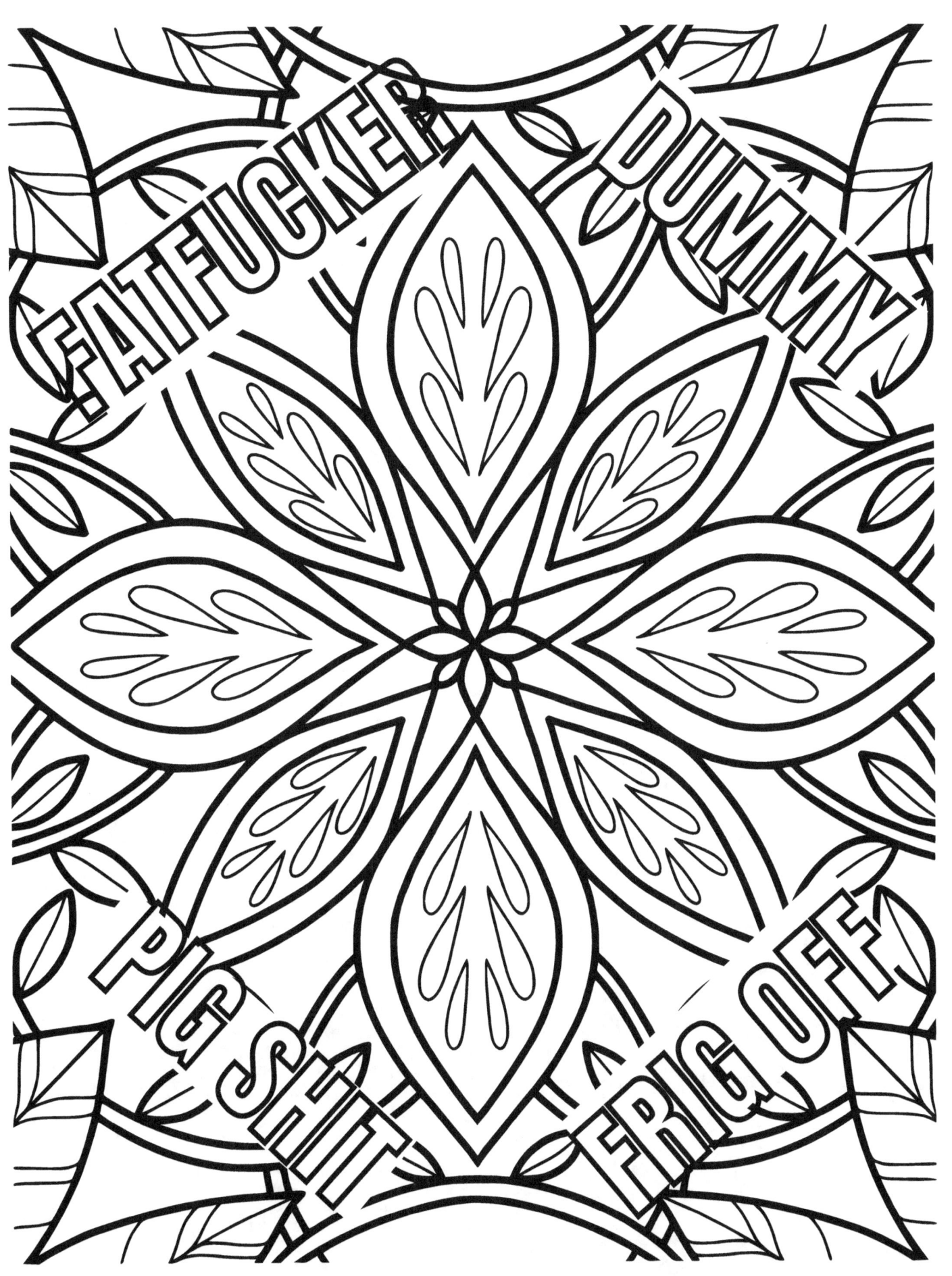

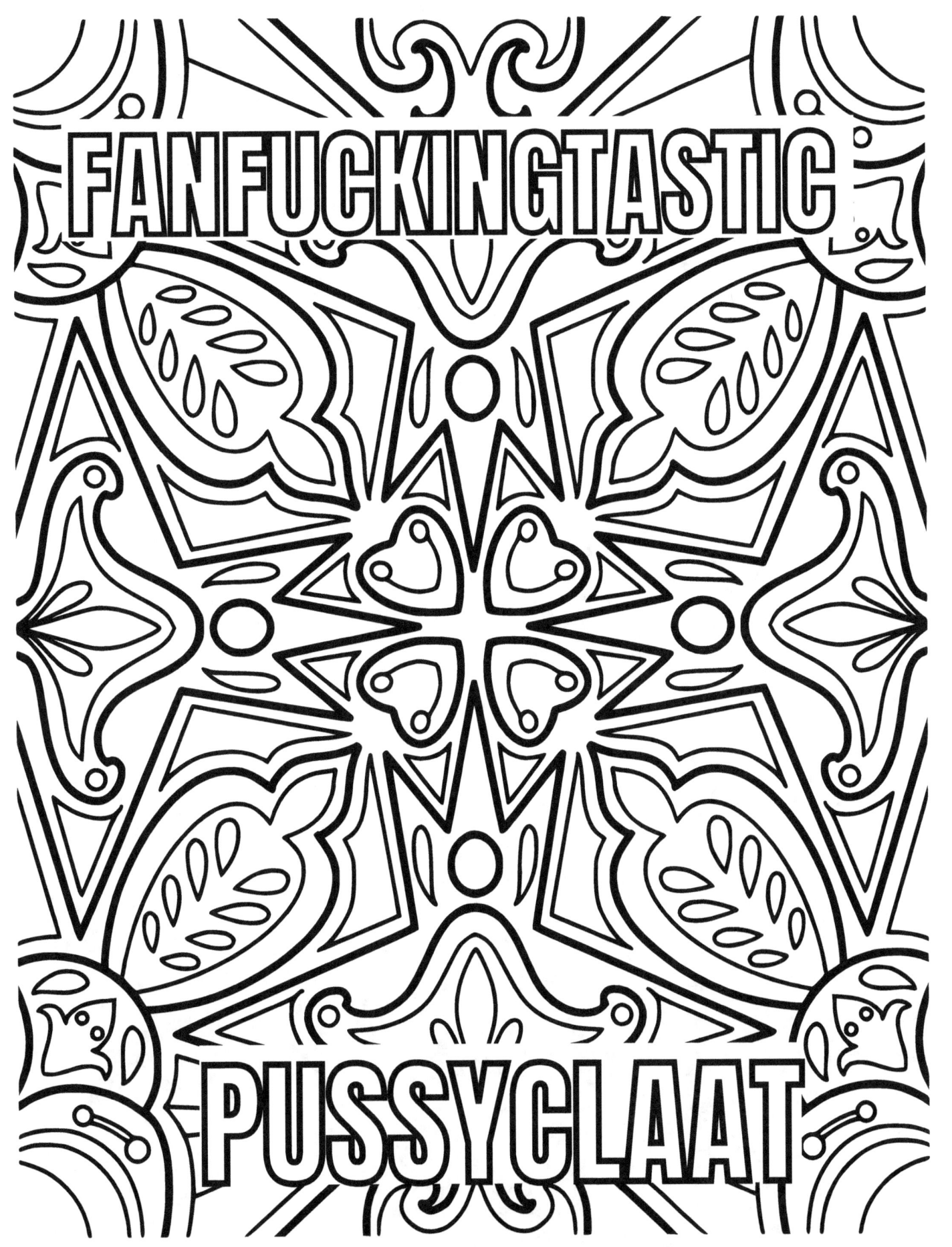

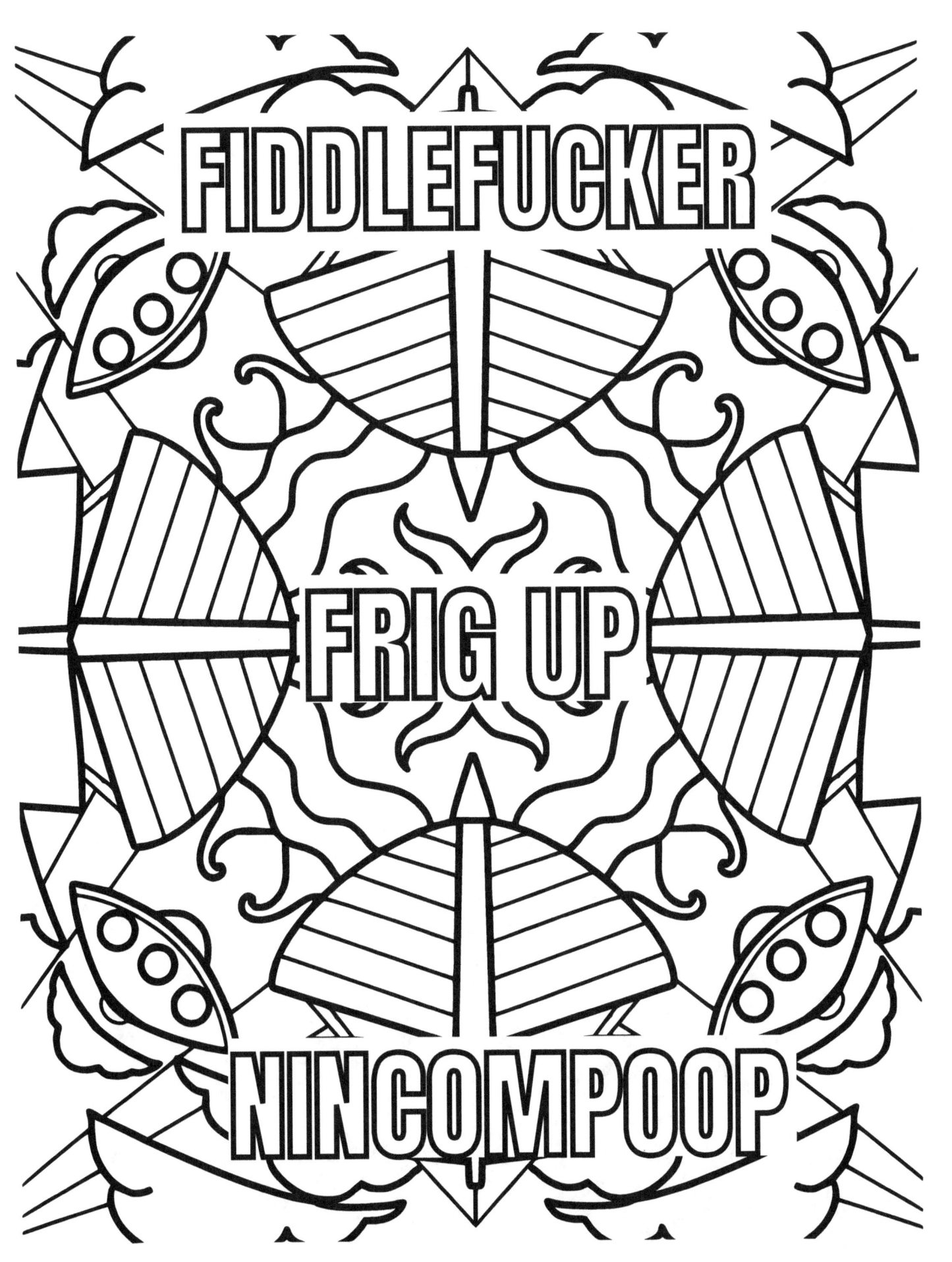

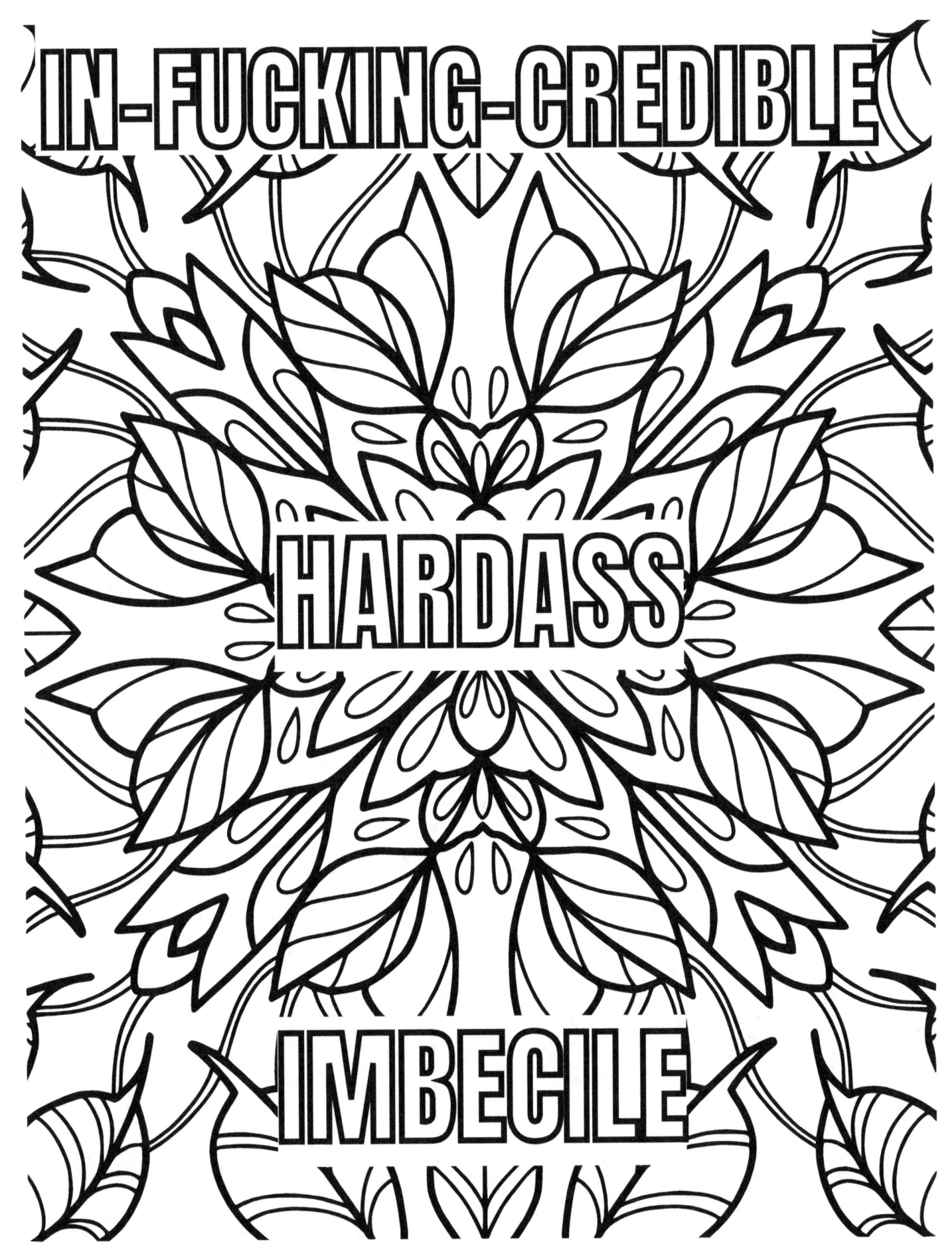

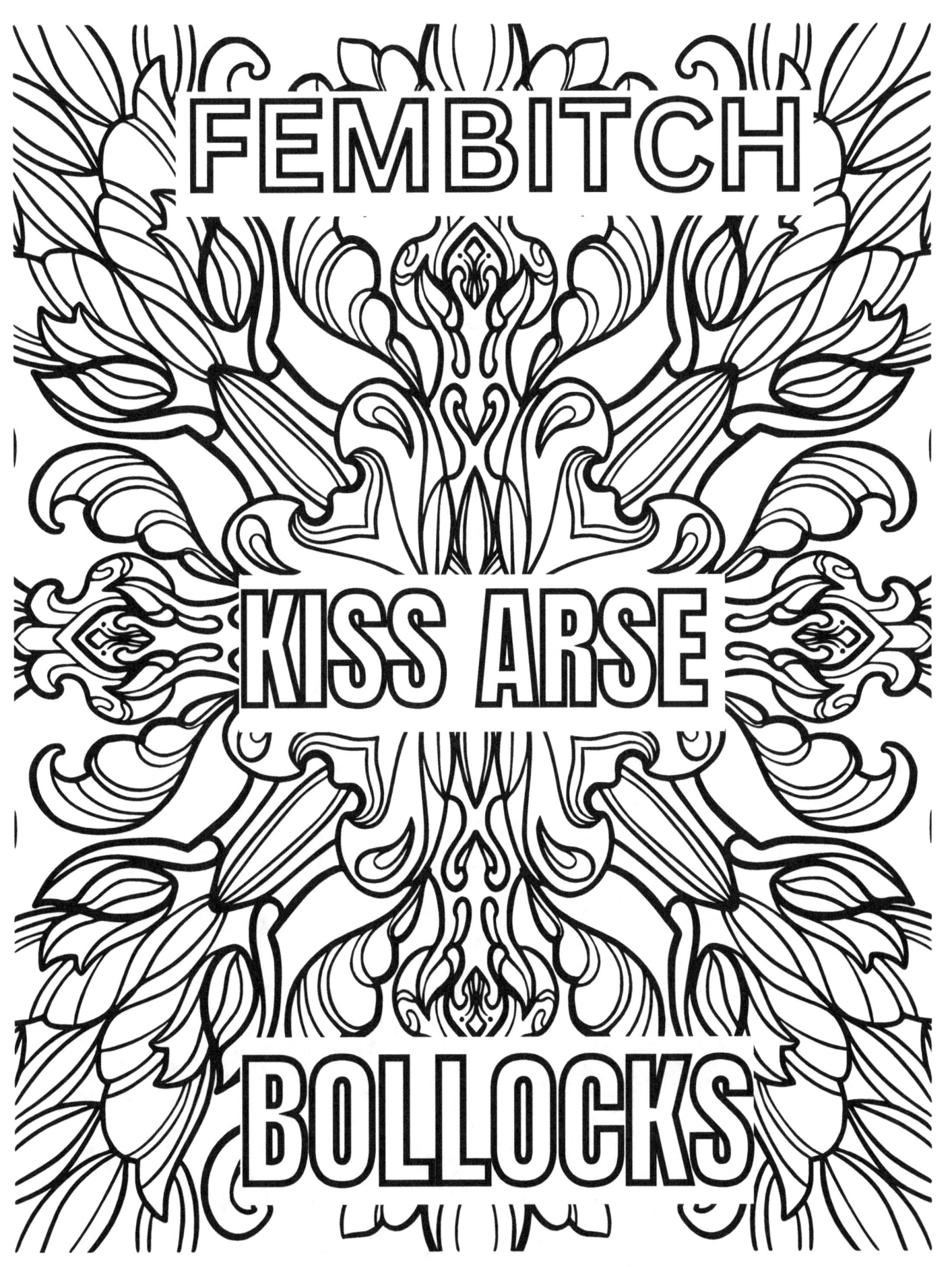

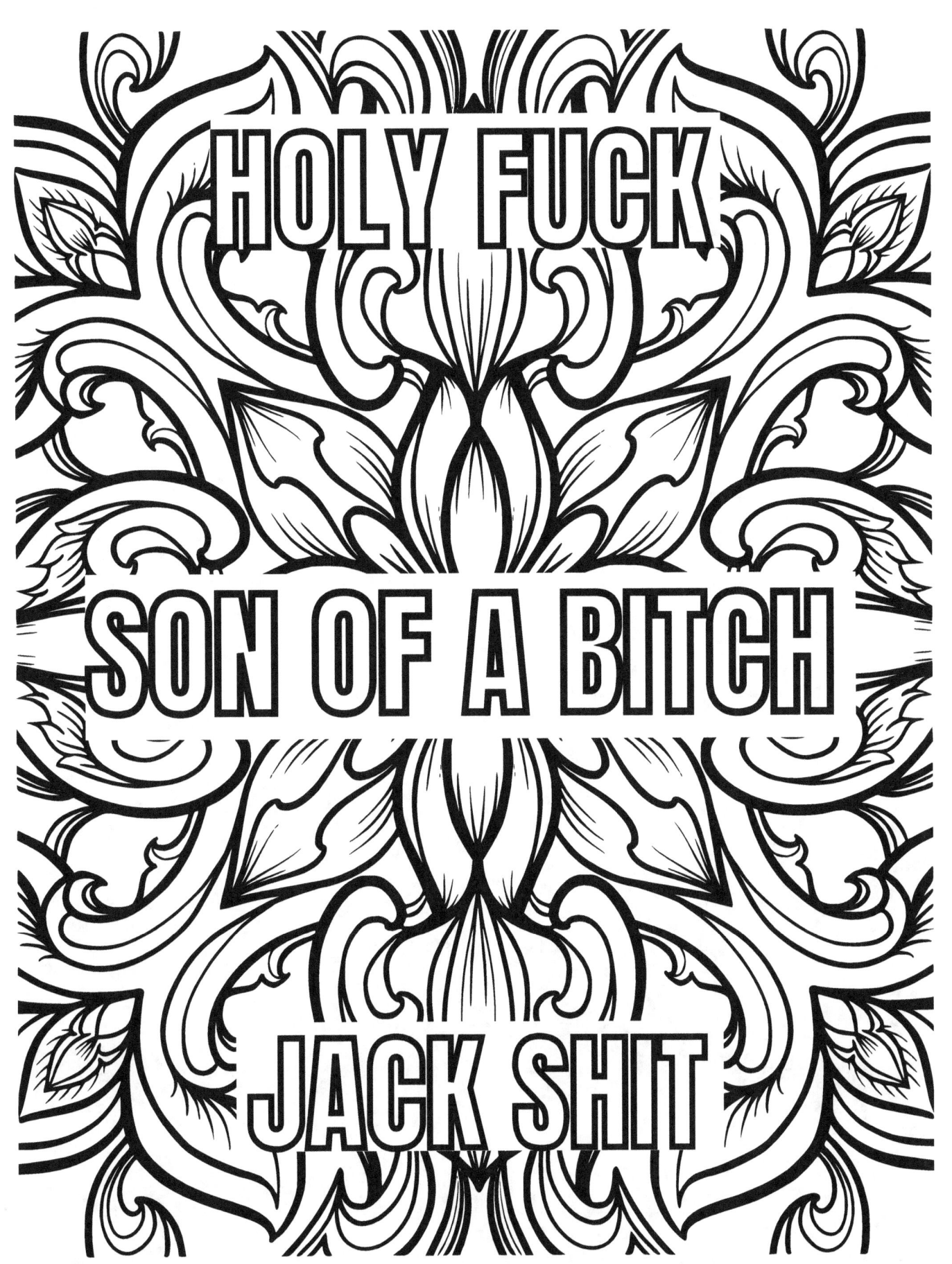

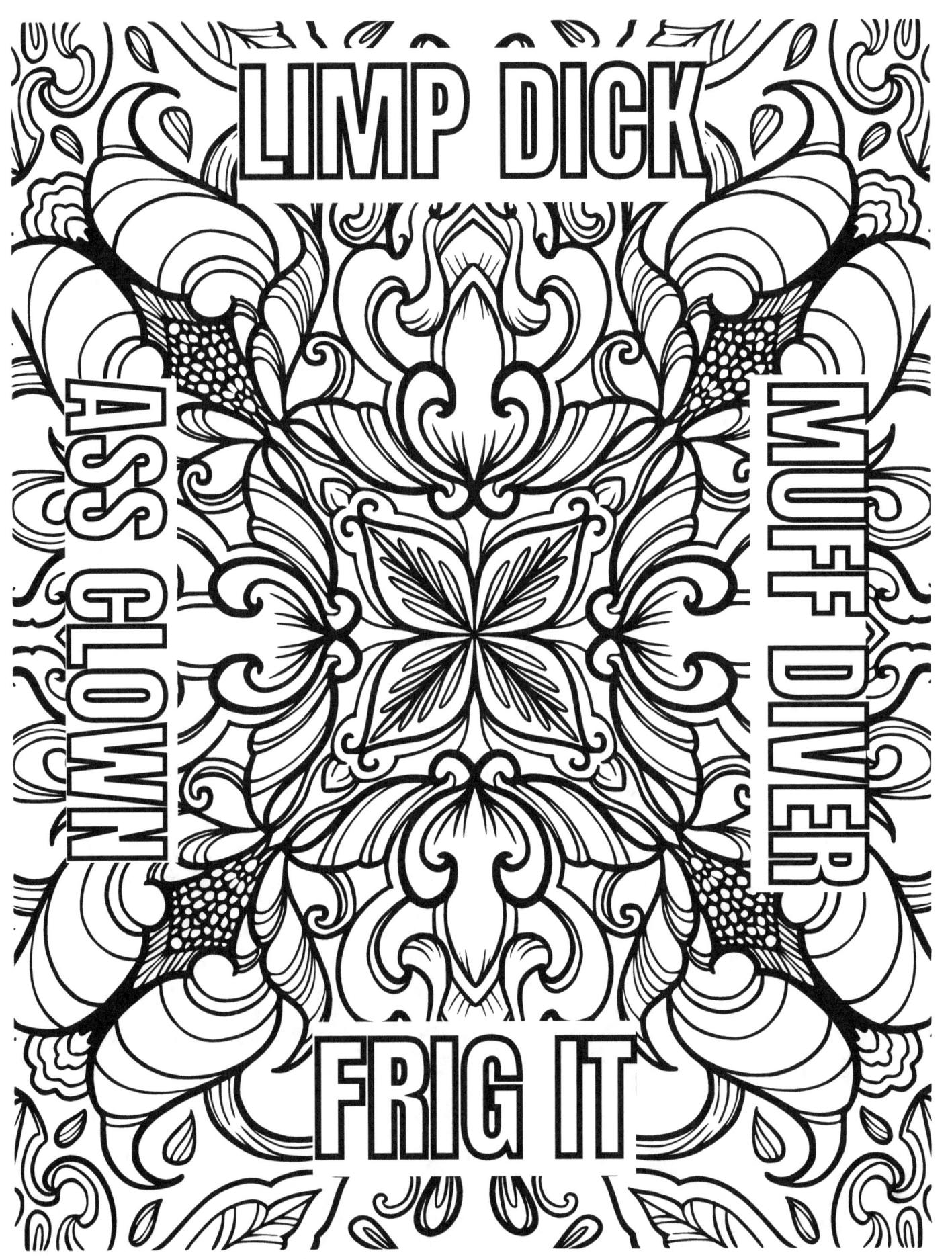

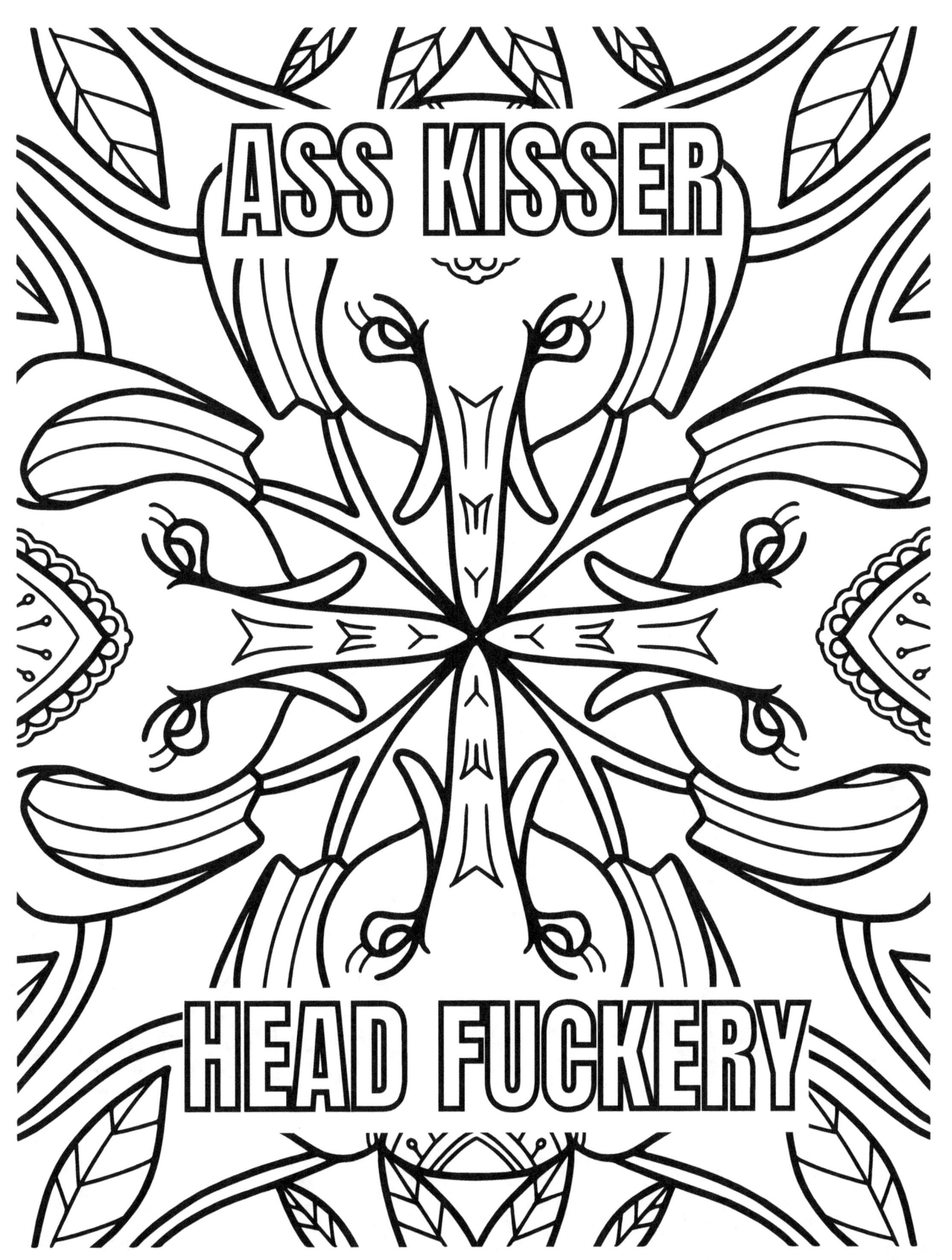

www.ingramcontent.com/pod-product-compliance
Lightning Source LLC
Chambersburg PA
CBHW060430220526
45465CB00008B/3085